RUSH!

THE MAKING OF A CLIMATE ACTIVIST

Tamsin Omond

MARION BOYARS

LONDON • NEW YORK

Published in Great Britain in 2009 by
MARION BOYARS PUBLISHERS LTD
24 Lacy Road London SW15 1NL
www.marionboyars.co.uk

Distributed in Australia by Tower Books Pty Ltd,
Unit 2, 17 Rodborough Road, Frenchs Forest, NSW 2086, Australia

Printed in 2009
10 9 8 7 6 5 4 3 2 1
Copyright © Tamsin Omond 2009
All rights reserved.

A CIP catalogue record for this book is available from the British Library.

ISBN 978-0-7145-3146-5

Baskerville 10pt/14pt
Printed in England by J.F. Print Ltd., Sparkford

RUSH!

THE MAKING OF A CLIMATE ACTIVIST

Tamsin Omond

MARION BOYARS
LONDON • NEW YORK

ACKNOWLEDGMENTS

This is the bit where I admit that some of the stories in this book have been blurred by memory and written as fact. Some names have been changed, some of the people I've met have merged into one and others are as true to life as I could write them. I'm sorry if you're surprised to see yourself written about here without warning, but I also thank you because it's your story that has made mine and I hope that ours might inspire others.

This is also the place where I thank the people who made this book happen: Plane Stupid; the Camp for Climate Action; the incredible women who give up whatever time they can to change their world with the Climate Rush; Deborah – editor extraordinaire and future leader of the world; Sasha for her guru-like status; Laetitia and Catheryn for saying yes; Chris and Jennifer for giving me hope; Mum and Dad for giving me faith, Emily for making me look talented; Alice for making me look fierce; Ben for making me look smart; Will for making me look good and Jessi for making me happy.

'I dedicate this book to where we are now, to climate change
and the possibility it presents, to all of the women
who are doing something to change their world,
and to my Granny who helped change mine.'

CONTENTS

CHAPTER ONE

THERE ARE DAYS WHEN I JUST WANT TO GO BACK.

The past is a big place but I guess if I had to put a date on the point at which things changed it'd be about summer '06. That was the year when everyone's clunky white iPod was playing 'Smile' and James Blunt was pissing off the whole country and making his name in rhyming slang. My second year exams weren't important. My biggest worries were whether I should keep kissing my ex and how to somehow get my hands on a Bestival ticket so I could be part of my friend's rainbow costume troupe. I remember the sun shining, getting a good tan and being wound up by *The God Delusion*. That summer was also the last time I flew.

I was saving for my summer trip, working on a market stall a couple of times a week. It was breaking the rules to work during term time but I managed to read a lot hiding in between the racks of clothes and nobody ever caught me. I still think it was the best job I've ever had – maybe the best I ever will have – though there's not much to compare it to: washing people's hair; working in a pretentious cocktail bar; typing up hymn sheets. It was great because the market stall owners knew me and I could almost always get free food. I'm a bit of a sucker for free food. Last year, when I was really, really skint, I became amazingly good at asking people in restaurants for their leftovers. Doing that now would make me cringe, but I still think it's stupid how much we waste.

I spent most of the summer cat-sitting for my English tutor, Dr Jessica Martin. She was a practising priest, but you wouldn't have known it unless you were up on a Sunday morning and saw her setting off in her dog-collar. I've heard her tell people about the first time she lectured me. I guess she wants to keep me in my place: she knows that I can take myself far too seriously. It was my first day of lectures and I was stressed out and hung-over. I arrived five minutes late – great start. As I sidled into the packed room, as quietly as I could, the class was already reading a poem. I took a handout and started racking my brains for something clever to say. The poem was about being a trickster. It was about saying one thing and doing the other; about misleading people with words.

Dr Martin looked up. 'Any comments, queries, ideas?'

Silence.

We all looked around wondering who'd be the first person to

speak; the first person to risk making a mistake.

'You're studying English – don't be scared about saying something stupid,' said Dr Martin. She gave a wry smile. 'You're lucky to have chosen this subject. For better or worse, almost anything goes.'

I like being the first person to speak. I don't actually enjoy forming the sentences but I do love the kudos that comes with biting the bullet, swallowing my fear and uttering an idea into the silence. On our first day of lectures, I'd be known as the girl who spoke first. I raised my hand. Jessica nodded at me.

'I think it's interesting that the rhymes themselves are tricky. The words don't quite rhyme but they look as though they should. You stumble over the end of the line – it doesn't trip off the tongue. Like "red" and "misled" [I pronounced it "myzled"]. They look as though they might rhyme, but then it doesn't quite fit. "Myzled" doesn't rhyme with "red".'

'But the word's not "myzled", it's "mis-led". Tamsin, it's a perfect rhyme.'

Jessica still laughs when she tells people this story, teasing me about wanting to enter academia when I couldn't even pronounce a simple word like 'misled'. That was the good thing about the market stall: Dixy – my boss – really didn't care about that sort of thing. The breezy marketplace was an escape from the hushed tension of the library, or the claustrophobia of dusty rooms where even dustier men frowned when they glimpsed my bare feet under the desk. The marketplace, the summer sun – totally stress-free.

From behind the clothes racks, book in hand, I watched the life of the city pass by. The trendies strode along in leggings and gypsy skirts, but my friends would visit the stall to see if there was anything worth buying second-hand. I'd spend the mornings sorting through bin-liners of crumpled clothes and always put aside the good stuff. One morning, I found three dead ferrets in a bin-bag. I suppose they were meant to be worn as scarves but their little faces, complete with teeth and staring eyes, really put me off. My friend Apoc, always fascinated by the macabre, loved them. I sold him the lot for £10 and I'm still regretting it. He hasn't lost them, or got tired of having their little hands clawing at his neck.

One tutor knew what I was up to. He'd come and visit me when he was at the farmers' market, and sing the praises of local food, though he once gave me an apple he'd bought there and I found a Waitrose supermarket sticker on its side. He'd smile if he caught me reading on duty, but still seemed worried that my 'giddy' lifestyle would end in my failing my degree. I suppose he saw the merit of sitting outside in the sun, selling second-hand clothes, but he also thought that perhaps I should be doing more, setting my sights higher.

One week I told him that I was doing the 'milk round', where city firms ply you with expensive alcohol and try and persuade you that working for £10 an hour, seventy hours a week, makes for a fulfilling life. I guess it's easy to be cynical now but at the time I did find it quite appealing. It was the women really, how smooth and polished they were. I was a bit in awe of them, even if they probably didn't deserve it. I went for some drinks at an advertising agency, with my friend Emily, and this woman with hair so immaculate it looked like a wig asked us why we were interested in the firm. I said something inane like, 'I'm really interested in brand recognition,' which sounded particularly dull when Emily came out with:

'I want to be able to manipulate people.'

The woman said 'Oh!' with a startled look on her face. She clearly liked Emily's abrupt honesty though, and spent most of the evening next to us, chatting about her New York flat and her *Sex and the City* lifestyle. It helped that she was really beautiful, her life seemed exciting and glamorous and I forgot that I was mostly there to eat the canapés. The next day, hung-over and trying to concentrate on Chaucer, the market stall seemed small and provincial. I was ambitious; I wanted to be successful; I wanted to make my mark on the world.

But I still had a year to work things out. The possibility of a city job was not going to disappear (or so we all thought) and for now, what mattered was working on the market stall until I had earned enough money for my holiday to Spain. My friend Charlie and I had booked our flights to Jerez. We planned to be there for a month, travelling around, and before we left we wanted to raise at least £300. The flights had only cost £30 return and we were taking a tent and planned to travel cheap, but I knew that once you start travelling you can never anticipate where you'll end up, or how much money you wish you had brought.

As it was, the only good thing about that flight was the price. At Stansted Airport, we were greeted by news of a terrorist threat. Our flight was delayed by ten hours and at the security check all our liquids were confiscated (no contact lens solution that night). Then when we finally got to Spain it turned out that our luggage had been lost. It was like the universe was trying to tell me something.

Charlie wasn't that bothered. He bought me some sun-screen and a hideous pair of shades and suggested we take the boat to Morocco and spend a month sleeping outside. We passed the night beneath the Castillo, woke up to a free shower from the sprinklers and caught the boat to Tangiers. We spent the month taking long, sweaty walks and sleeping out under the stars. We dropped into a festival and I nearly drowned when I took a drunken swim in the strong currents that swirled around that part of the coast. We watched the World Cup final in an Italian restaurant which served awful food, but also endless illicit alcohol when Italy won. An old Eritrean guy tried to tell me his life story in pidgin Italian. I found him impossible to understand, until he brought out his hashish and it suddenly began to make a lot more sense. I remember walking through the streets at five in the morning hand-in-hand with Charlie – my 'husband' while we were there – and feeling dizzy at the coincidences that had brought this strange group of people together for a few short hours on a hot Moroccan night.

There are days when I just want to go back. It's crazy, really, the difference that cheap flights made, how quickly they opened up the world and made it feel like flying is something we all have this right to. Now I've closed that world and sometimes it can feel like I've given up so much, the thousands of places I'll never see and thousands of experiences I'll never have...but there's definitely a pay off. Weekend trips to Italy or my Gran's house in Prague are things of the past, but taking slower journeys on hulking, Soviet trains in Eastern Europe, or setting off on a bike with a backpack and feeling this total sense of independence – experiences like that start to change your whole concept of travel. The idea of being on the rainy tarmac at Luton Airport one minute and out in the Ibizan sun a few short hours later begins to seem really unnatural, as though by moving at that speed you end up leaving something really important behind. It was definitely hardest at the beginning, watching my friends jet off round the world and wishing I could just forget about climate change for a bit and pretend that my choices didn't matter. But then I'd think about all the places they were missing as they travelled above the clouds at 500 miles an hour, and what they would get to see if they just slowed down and kept their feet a little closer to the ground. And the longer I live this way of life, and the greater the distance between now and my last flight, the more I recognise what I have gained and the journeys and adventures still to come, and the more excited I get by the plans my friends and I speak about, on so many nights as planes pass high overhead: the things we'll see when we go overland to India, one day.

***

At the end of that summer, as the new term began, I met Alice. She's married to a famous poet, Geoffrey Hill, and when I heard she'd been hired as college chaplain, he was the one I wanted to meet. I'd written a dissertation on him and I thought that maybe I could be his protégé. I helped them move into their new house, I guess hoping to impress him, but by the time I'd finished arranging their bookshelves I'd realised that it was Alice who would change my life. She's the most unexpected priest I've ever met. She isn't nice (at least not in that way that means nothing more than sweet and dull), she doesn't pat people comfortingly and she doesn't mince her words. She's American and Jewish and on a mission to pull people into the church. I'd pretty much given up on Christianity after a bad experience at the start of university, but she managed to reconnect me with the kind of love and acceptance my grandparents had shown me.

Both of my grandparents had removable body parts. Grandad's eye was shot out before WWII. When we were much younger, he'd take his glass eye out at bath-time, put it by the sink and go to check the stove. He knew how to keep us under control: 'I'm watching, y'know.' Granny had her breast cut off, a mastectomy. When we went swimming in freezing waters off the north-west coast of Scotland, she would pull the plastic cup from where it lay against the gap in her chest. The gesture was so honest and so vulnerable. She would watch us all as we looked at her with embarrassment and with a shameful hint of disgust. Her gaze was straightforward – not proud, but definitely focused. She was dying, but she shrugged off the helplessness and futility of it. Instead she had a lust for life and an acceptance of all that meant.

My earliest memory of her is of a telling-off. I was sitting on the bottom step outside her house gnawing on my thumbnail. It's a habit I still have. I was nervous: it was the night of my granddad's seventieth birthday and we were going to perform a play about his life. My mum had written it and for one scene I was going to be Granny. I'd interrogate him and ask him where our lives were heading next... 'I know, why don't we turn our land into a charity for people with disabilities and their carers? We can call it "Holton Lee".' When I said this line I had to be as inspired and inspirational as my granny. I had to say it with such passion that my husband would believe that giving the best of his land away to create a charity was a perfectly reasonable thing to do.

I sat on the step, chewing my nail and wondering how she'd managed it. Then she found me and she told me off. Everyone inside was working hard, preparing food and washing cutlery. Why was I hiding outside and biting at my fingers? There was a lot to do and I was being no help at all. I remember feeling grumpy, upset that she hadn't shown me her 'inspirational' side. But once I was in the kitchen I was soon distracted and stopped worrying about the play. Later I realised her rescuing me from the step where I had been alone and outside the family buzz showed just how well she knew me.

About twenty years before, Granny and Grandad had used their home as a base for a Christian community. By the time I could remember anything this had become 'Post Green Camp', a week of childhood bliss every spring, every year. This was when my brothers, cousins and I would vie for Granny's attention. We could see the awe and respect other people felt for her. She bossed us about, telling us to chop vegetables, fetch water or simply get out of her way. She taught us that we were only as helpless as we were alone, and in a world so full, and so small, there was never good reason to feel at a loss. Later, the land where the camp was held was transformed into Holton Lee, the charity sprung from her vision. It exists still, growing year by year, a place where people with disabilities and the people who care for them can have a break from a world designed for 'normal' people.

As my gran's cancer spread she eventually lost the part of her throat that gave her a voice. Instead she held something underneath her chin, which felt the vibrations of what she was trying to say and transformed her silent mouthing into a robotic buzz. We were told that it would not be long before she died. She had a special place in Scotland where she'd go each summer. The whole family would visit her at the same time. I wasn't there for her last summer: a friend had invited me to go to Thailand. It seemed the opportunity of a lifetime and no-one could persuade me otherwise. Shortly after I returned, Granny died. I don't think it would have occurred to her to be scared, helpless or lonely, but I do wish that she'd had all of her grandchildren around her for that holiday.

It's tricky to explain how someone I find so hard to sum up in words can have had such an influence on everything that I have ever wanted to think, say or be. If there is a heaven then at its gate will be my Granny, Faith, no longer wracked with cancer, holding a key and waiting for me to explain my life.

But I had wandered from the church, and it took meeting Alice ten years later to bring me back. She did it in the simplest way possible, by giving me a weekly routine and a job to do. Every Sunday I just had to turn up ten minutes before the service, put on a cassock and a surplus, carry a cross to the altar, and help the priest prepare communion. After the service we would all go and eat breakfast. That was it. Alice's minimal requirements made her seem very different to the other Christians I'd met when I first arrived. No praying out loud for people I did not know. No public confessions. Just a routine of worship and a quiet part for me to play.

On Sunday afternoons, Alice and I took walks together and talked about the future. We shared some similar ideas about the Church, ideas that I'd been thinking about on my own for ages. It didn't seem all that complicated to either of us: love God, love your neighbour, make spirituality relevant, don't exclude people. Sometimes on these walks we seemed to solve the world's problems, starting with the church, and I began to feel like I would have a place in it, like my opinions mattered. Towards the end of university, a job opportunity came up, to shadow a priest in a North London parish. Since I had met Alice, the allure of the slick city women had diminished. The market stall was a dream from a time when I didn't feel I had a purpose. Making money could wait. For three months I worked non-stop for my finals, pausing only to watch *Neighbours* and laugh at Paris Hilton's jailbird antics, and then suddenly university was over. I had a calling. I'd work with a priest for a year and maybe, for that year, I'd do some good.

***

My job title was 'Parish Administrator and Pastoral Assistant'. I had to type and fold three hundred service sheets a week, and at Easter, Christmas and other important church days I typed and folded thousands more. I filled in the baptism register, and every now and then, the ones for funerals and marriages too. I spent every morning from nine until noon in a church office built into the nave of the church. When I closed the doors I could see and hear the services and I had to remember to put my phone on silent. Nobody wants the moment when the bread becomes the body of Christ to be interrupted by a ringing phone, a muttered, 'Oh shit!' and a thud as it's grabbed from its hiding place.

The fun side of my job was my pastoral duties, when I got to come out from behind my desk, walk through the dark cool of the nave, and step into the outside world. There are a lot of people who depend upon the church. Every week one of our priests would take communion at the local hospice, performing the ritual for the old and the sick, talking and listening for hours. The church where I was working was renowned for engaging with the local kids. The youth groups and people that led them were not at all evangelical. You didn't have to be a Christian to come and hang out in the church, go to a recording studio with the youth team or spend a week outside London learning adventure sports. I really liked that. I'd never understood the division between the church and the rest of the world, and I was always cautious about churches that catered for Christians and Christians alone. I like to think that the visions written in small stories at the end of a very old book are about more than separate communities worshipping in isolation, judging the big bad world outside.

One week, I made a new friend after Tuesday Tea. She was sitting at the very back of church with her head down, exhausted. Tuesday

Teas were monthly events held for the elderly of the community. We provided entertainment and a silver tea service for an afternoon. Doris, one of the more fragile church-goers, was leaning on her stick and waiting for a taxi to arrive to take her home. It had been a long afternoon and she was frustrated.

'I called them. I'm sure I did. Oh, I don't know.'

I knelt in front of her and asked if she had a number for the firm. I called and they had no record of the order, but said a taxi would be there in about fifteen minutes. By the time it arrived, Doris and I were friends. We'd been chatting about the previous week's service, and about Easter, which was approaching fast. I knew something about her life, but didn't want to pry. Instead I talked to her about climate change and we agreed that the weather was definitely not what it used to be. She made her way slowly to the street and into the taxi. I asked whether she wanted me to come along too but she said no.

'Oh dear, I don't want to trouble you.'

It was no trouble at all but I was embarrassed to push so I suggested that I visit her the following Tuesday afternoon.

The next week I made my way to Camden, wondering whether I should buy her some flowers, or perhaps a cake. But of course, I'd left my wallet at home. By the canal I found a lone daffodil. It was a pity to pick it, but I had a feeling it'd be appreciated and so I broke its stem and kept on walking.

Doris lived in a small flat on a council estate. I walked past a group of boys sitting on the gate. They were smoking something and generally taking the piss. As I went past they whistled and I shook my daffodil at them.

I knocked on her door and the net curtains went up. Doris peered at me through her kitchen window and so I lifted the letterbox and called inside:

'Doris, it's Tamsin, from the church.' I felt like a Jehovah's Witness.

Three minutes later she'd opened the door and was beckoning me in. She led me to her living room where several tarts had been laid out carefully on the table and a pot of tea was brewing. I felt my heart hit the back of my chest. The sunshine was pouring in through the window and she had a great view of London, laid out below. I wondered how often she made it out of this room and into the world outside. She was extremely fragile. I decided that I'd start bringing the world to her. I went to the kitchen, found a tall glass, filled it with water and put in the daffodil I'd brought. I put it on her mantelpiece and sat down.

'Eat, eat,' she said and so I did.

It's hard to remember what we spoke about that day. She told me stories about her family, a daughter who had died from cancer, a grandson on a gap year in Australia, far away. He texted her from time to time (I grinned at the thought of her tapping out messages on her mobile phone) and his father printed off the email updates he sent. We talked for two hours, when I had thought I'd only want to stay for one. I loved telling her everything I'd been up to and hearing her life story.

I'm just one of many parishioners who has spent time with someone old, viewing it as a 'Christian duty', and been surprised by the friendship they have found. My visit resulted in a strange and special relationship built between two people from different generations, who found that they had more than a little in common, and who both appreciated each other's kindness. Doris had lived a tough life, yet she was incredibly resilient. We set up a routine. Every fortnight I went to see Doris, ate the custard tarts that she bought for me, drank tea, chatted church politics, washed up and left. She was a little nervous, as if she thought it might be a hassle for me, and I was just the same, not wanting to tire her or put her out. We saw each other in church and felt conspiratorial, like we were having secret meetings, belonging to no-one else but us.

But as the months passed and I folded my service sheets, making any contribution I could to the lives of the parishioners around me, I watched the news and read the papers and became uneasy about the ever-growing threat of climate change. For some time I'd been wondering whether I was on the right path. In my final year at university, on the same weekends when I was taking long walks with Alice, I was also reading books on climate science, fed to me by the two activists I lived with. They were terrified about the future and pretty soon I started seeing their point of view. I guess I'd always known that change was coming, but I hadn't realised how soon, or how bad it was going to be. Gradually I became aware that we were sitting on all these time bombs – the risks of a 2°C temperature rise, the shrinking ice of the arctic sea, the growth of aviation, massive deforestation – and that ticking clock started to inform everything about my life. I couldn't stop thinking about these facts, I couldn't shut up about the time bombs and I just couldn't prioritise my job.

⌛ TIME BOMB: *What's with the 2°C ?*

On the floor of my sitting room, I read about a 2°C rise in world temperatures. This is what the International Panel on Climate Change (the IPCC) decided might be a 'safe' level of global warming, back in the early 1990s. They say that since the industrial revolution and our discovery that by burning fossil fuels we could create almost limitless energy, global temperatures have increased by 0.8°C. It's crazy – less than two hundred years ago we discovered fossil fuels and now we're all so hooked that our lives would be unimaginable without the option of jumping in the car for that trip to the shops, turning up the gas when the weather outside is cold, eating food that has been transported by plane to your supermarket. Everything that we do increases the amount of carbon dioxide in the atmosphere which creates further climate change and a higher global temperature: 0.8°C... Well, it might not sound like much, but I was shocked when I realised that we were already seeing its effects:

- Glaciers retreating in the Himalayas and massive shrinking of the Arctic sea ice.
- Drought in Australia.
- $150 billion a year of damage from natural catastrophes.
- Floods in Bangladesh which put 80% of the country under 2m of water.
- Temperature rises of 3-4°C in Alaska.
- Sea-level rises of 3.1mm per year since 1993.
- 300,000 extra deaths a year from higher temperatures, which cause the spread of disease.

As the temperature rises, the situation gets worse. These facts really scare me:

- When we go over 1°C (that's a 'when' not an 'if') there'll be no ice on Mount Kilimanjaro, the ecosystem around the Great Barrier Reef will completely collapse and hundreds

of island nations will be uninhabitable.
- If we reach 2°C the World Wildlife Fund thinks the Greenland ice sheet will go into meltdown. This would result in a 7m sea level rise, putting most coastal cities under water.
- 3°C will see the Amazon ecosystem collapse, making it the greatest emitter of CO_2 in the world, as trees die and forest fires rage through the landscape.

2°C is just a number that was picked out of the air. Some people point out that because of feedback loops (like the Arctic sea ice – a time bomb in itself) the 0.8°C rise we've already had may well already be past the 'safe limit' anyway. We might not be able to stop climate chaos now, but pumping more and more CO_2 into the atmosphere is almost definitely going to make it worse. If we cut our emissions as much as we can, it won't stop global warming, but it's the only hope we have of avoiding a total climate catastrophe.

In church I was outspoken about the role that I felt Christians should play in the fight against climate change. The vicar, my boss, became concerned that environmental campaigning was dominating my parish work. He asked me to go and speak with him one evening in late February.

As I approached his door, I already knew that he was right. The life of a priest is not a life of campaigns. It is a quiet life of service to a community. It is a very special sort of life. There are divisions in the Church of England and these quarrels attract headlines and controversy, but in reality the church isn't made up of the opinions of prominent people, just as society isn't made up of the things that politicians say. The life of a church is the mundane routine it offers a community, the cool sanctuary of an empty building on a busy high street or the priest in the vicarage who will always take your call. During those six months I had fallen in love with the community that the church offered. There were disagreements, of course, but they tended to be personality clashes or misunderstandings and the controversies about sexuality and gender that concerned church leaders didn't seem to matter day-to-day. Personal disagreements could always be solved, because in a community harmony isn't about forcing uniformity – it's about resolving conflicts with compromise and forgiving love.

I knocked quietly on the door of the office. I felt sorry for the people I'd neglected, and for the three-week gap since I'd last seen Doris. I hadn't been concentrating on serving the parish. I had been too distracted trying to turn it green. Now I would have to tell my priest some sort of lie since tomorrow I couldn't be at work – instead I would be with the protest group Plane Stupid, climbing the roofs of Parliament.

Why We Can Trust Science On This One

There's been a lot of confusion about climate change. Some of it has been real scientific debate, a lot of it has been generated by paid-up climate deniers funded by Exxon Mobile, who wanted to rock people's faith in science so that they'd buy more cigarettes. (Crazy but true – George Monbiot's book *Heat: How to Stop the Planet Burning* tells the whole story.)

It's true that science never gives absolute certainties. Instead, it gives probabilities, identifying events which have occurred so many times that it's really unlikely that something different will happen. These probabilities have allowed us to build skyscrapers, cure cancer, genetically modify plants and have test-tube babies. Of course, we shouldn't accept science blindly. It has its limits. But our whole world is also based on its principles and it's our best hope of predicting and controlling the future.

The world's climate is so complex that it takes huge amounts of computer power to model it. These models are full of problems and oversimplifications, but there are some things we know for sure (ie: lots of people have done the same experiment and found the same results). One is that the level of carbon dioxide in the atmosphere, after being stable for a really long time, has been rising for the last two hundred years.

Carbon dioxide is an important part of the greenhouse effect

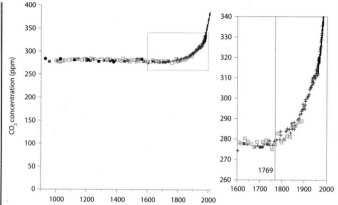

Figure 1.4. Carbon dioxide (CO_2) concentrations (in parts per million) for the last 1100 years, measured from air trapped in ice cores (up to 1977) and directly in Hawaii (from 1958 onwards). 1769 is the year James Watts invented the steam engine (from *Sustainable Energy: Without Hot Air* by David Mackay (2008)).

– the way that heat from sunlight is trapped on earth, making it warm enough for life. Because the system was stable for so long even the small rise in CO_2 has made a big difference. Over the same time period global temperatures have been rising.

It's not that other things don't make a difference. Sunspots affect the temperature on earth. Sulphur emissions banned twenty years ago are still high in the atmosphere, blocking sunlight and helping cool the earth. Things change year to year, and there are huge climate cycles. But the weather is visibly changing. The arctic sea ice may be gone in a couple of summers' time – that's ice that has been there for three million years. It's possible that climate change is not man-made, that our emissions have nothing to do with rising temperatures. It's possible, but not at all likely – and our whole civilisation is built on doing the thing that seems most likely. If a doctor tells us we only have a 10% chance of surviving cancer without chemotherapy almost everyone would get treated. Why don't we trust climate scientists just because they're only 95% sure climate change is man-made?

One last thing: beneath any article on the environment you'll find someone, if not ten people, telling you that climate change is a huge conspiracy. They're usually confused about who is behind it – one day it's communists, the next hippies or the UN – but they are totally certain that all the science is a hoax, that climate change isn't happening, that if it is it wasn't man-made, or if it was man-made it'll all be fine because we'll get a nice tan.

I can't tell you how much I wish they were right.

When the global leaders first met in the early 90s to discuss climate change they wanted to keep emissions at 1990 levels. Rather than rising by 1.1% a year, CO_2 levels wouldn't rise at all – a growth rate of 0%. Last year they grew by 3%. If this is a big conspiracy it's a pretty unsuccessful one. I'd say that the power lies with those who are trying to say that emissions don't matter, not the other way round.

CHAPTER TWO

I BELONG, WITH DIFFERENT LEVELS OF CONVICTION, TO a variety of groups. Being part of a group means giving something – your time, your money, your love – and getting something back in return. Some of the groups I belong to might seem more glamorous or more fun than others, and the sacrifices some demand might seem too high a price to pay if you don't quite understand what I get back from it. I guess I think there's something important in all of them.

When I'm whizzing around London on my bright yellow racing bike I am a member of the bike tribe. Made up of couriers and trendy East Londoners, this group likes to cut up taxis, race through red traffic lights, rely on a single gear and wear the latest in designer bike-wear. We're not friends and we don't chat whilst waiting at the traffic lights, but we do have mutual respect. We nod approvingly when someone manages to wind their way stylishly between two buses and an ambulance before cycling off at break-neck speed. We don't talk about our means of transport, or compare reasons for choosing this particular way of getting around, but we do share assumptions. There should be fewer cars on the road. Public transport in London is way too expensive. We should all get a little more active.

But if you're part of a group then you'd better be ready to encounter opposition. I'm biking down Oxford Street when a boy breaks off from his crew, stands at the side of the road and yells 'OFF' as I speed past. Two weeks earlier I'd been in East London and as I approached a group of men they jumped into the road so that I swerved and narrowly missed falling off, before pedalling away fast. I suppose I can't expect everyone to share my reverence for the pedal-powered.

As part of the Church of England you encounter some opposition too. Richard Dawkins isn't the only one who seems to have a vendetta against Christianity. There are also the divisions within the church itself, with some people thinking the most important part of the religion is social justice, and others wanting to damn Jews, Muslims or gay people. There are those who want to exclude me and say that I don't belong in their community, and sometimes I don't know what to do with that.

When I'm talking with new friends about saving the world I'm one of the eco-activists. Sometimes this group seems even broader than the church, with members ranging from people who've turned away from society to live in sustainable communities, to political lobbyists who try to transform the mainstream. Most are vegetarian; many are vegan. Some have 'day jobs' which don't really relate to their environmental beliefs. Some of them, like Al Gore, still fly. I suppose there are lots of different levels of eco-activism. As with the church, I avoid those people who seem to think it's their job to decide who is 'in' and who is 'out', but I guess a line does need to be drawn somewhere.

I don't see activism as a lifestyle choice. To me, an eco-activist is the most mainstream thing you could possibly be. We're fighting for everybody – for everybody's right to food, to water, to a predictable climate, to clean air and electricity. But I know that most people don't see it that way. Many feel pretty alienated from the opinions of 'the greens'. I know that's how I felt when neither my present life nor my imagined future were particularly eco-friendly. My worthier friends would take long journeys by bus down the winding roads to my grandmother's home in Prague. I'd meet them from their two-day journey fresh from my two-hour flight. Of course I cared about the future of the world, but I never really believed that my decision not to fly, or to change my light bulbs, or recycle, was going to be the decision that really mattered. The stories that my environmentalist friends would tell about rising temperatures, melting ice-caps and ever-decreasing rainforests were probably true, but I hoped that the government would have it all in hand. After all, which politician was really going to blindly lead us into a climate catastrophe?

⧗ TIME BOMB: *Arctic Sea Ice*

In the summer of 2007, scientists monitoring the Arctic sea ice shocked the world with the pictures they produced. From one year to the next it had shrunk by 1.5 million square kilometres – that's an area nearly three times the size of France.

In some ways 2008 was even worse. The previous year there were perfect melting conditions – clear skies and high temperatures. 2008 was a lot cooler. The Arctic sea ice recovered a bit, but not much, even though the conditions were ideal for ice to grow, while it covered a larger area, it was thinner and so the total mass was actually the smallest it has ever been.

Just a couple of years ago the IPCC (Intergovernmental Panel on Climate Change) thought the Arctic would be ice-free in summer by the end of the century. The Climate Safety Report, published in 2008, now predicts there will be no sea ice by summer 2015, and this might even happen as early as 2011.

Losing the Arctic sea ice is a massive time bomb.

(See diagram on the next page.)

KEY

Water

Ice less than
5 years old

Ice more than
5 years old

MAP OF ARCTIC SEA ICE LOSS 1989 - 2007

- Ice is white and reflects sunlight. Water is darker and absorbs sunlight. The Arctic sea ice works like a huge fridge for the whole northern hemisphere and as it grows warmer the whole area will become warmer too.
- The permafrost in the Arctic Circle is frozen ground containing millions of tonnes of greenhouse gases. If it all melts it will triple the carbon dioxide in the atmosphere, massively increasing global warming.
- Even worse, it's not just CO_2 trapped in the ground – there are also tonnes and tonnes of methane, which is twenty-five times more powerful as a greenhouse gas! Although the sea ice won't cause a sea level rise by itself, it could lead to the irreversible decline of the Greenland ice sheet, leading to a 7m rise.

It may be too late to save the Arctic sea ice. We may have no choice but to try huge geo-engineering projects, like spraying sulphur high into the atmosphere to reflect sunlight, in order to make the ice form again. At this stage I think we have to consider every possible course of action, look at the risks, and make difficult choices; but we certainly can't pretend it isn't happening.

Right now, we have no international agreements to radically reduce carbon emissions, we have an economic crisis that has shifted public concern away from climate change and we have fewer than about eighty-six months to stop the planet warming. There's no overwhelmingly prominent social movement to focus our attention on the biggest ever threat to the planet and humanity. When scientists are ignored by the people who are supposed to be looking after our future it makes me want to march into town with a placard and a megaphone and shout: 'Watch out for climate chaos! The end is nigh!'

But that would be a lonely way to spend my days and it probably wouldn't be a lot of help. Judging by the fate of the solitary figure I see every time I go to Oxford Circus – placarded, megaphoned, extremely well-versed in some brand of Christianity and resolutely ignored – screaming on busy street corners is not the best way to make people pay attention. Don't wear your desperation on your sleeve and especially don't force it into the path of other people's shopping trips. Helplessness is a feeling we are all familiar with. Hearing someone else scream their despair gives us even more reason to keep our heads down and walk swiftly on. Telling us we're helpless is not going to make us feel better, and will never be the solution. The only way to work our way out of this mess is through asking for, and offering, help. There's only so much that a person can do alone. Together, though, if they're big enough, groups can change the world.

Since the economic crisis, it's become all too clear that no-one has our future in their hands. It was a crisis that was predicted by top economists, but politicians ignored the warnings, blindly hoping that it could be avoided, or at least put off until the end of their time in office. It was a crisis which anyone with any common sense could see coming. You can't just keep on building houses and selling them to people who are never going to be able to pay for them. You can't have infinite growth on a finite planet. Now the future is a little less certain – a lot less secure – we all have to become a bit better at taking that all-important first step, swallowing our pride, un-stiffening our upper lips and asking for help.

***

'Oi – can you lend a hand bringing the hay?'

He was definitely looking in my direction and almost certainly shouting to me.

I had been at the Heathrow Climate Camp in Sipson village for two hours. The bus from the nearest station, West Drayton, had been filled with people carrying the same sort of luggage: rucksacks, sleeping bags and tents. It was my first visit to Sipson, an 11th century village that, for the past fifty years, has been on the outskirts of Heathrow Airport. As Heathrow has grown, its perimeter fence has inched ever closer to Sipson. The airport's most recent expansion plan, a third runway, will involve demolishing Sipson and scattering its residents around the country. At the bus stop in the village centre we got out and joined the stream of people on their way to the camp.

We helped one another over the hay bale barricades. The first thing I saw as I stood cautiously on top of them, gripping a stranger's hand, were three long metal poles balanced against each other to make a huge tripod, holding a boy twenty metres high so he could hook up a banner which said 'THIS PLANET HAS NO EMERGENCY EXITS'. Below him stretched the camp: hundreds of coloured tents, marquees and groups of people walking on duck board footpaths carrying tent poles, tarpaulins or food. The gate where I entered was staffed by five people wearing orange bibs that read 'legal support'; behind them was the 'welcome tent', three wind-turbines and a row of compost toilets. The legal supporters asked whether we'd been stopped and searched on the way into the camp. We all had. Did the police bother to give us a reason? No, but we had all been presented with pink slips. 'Keep them,' the campers laughed, 'there's a competition on. First person to get to a hundred stop and search forms wins.' Smiles broke out across the group and we newcomers laughed too. It did seem a bit ridiculous that there were three policemen to every camper.

I'd pitched my tent and was about to have a proper look around when the boy called for help with the hay. He was lanky, with very pale arms protruding from a Kooks T-shirt. There was a bit of a chill in the air and I wondered how he was warm enough. I thought more hay must be needed at the gate, and so I ran over, happy to make a friend.

'Hey, I'm John.'

'Tamsin.' We shook hands.

'Right let's go and sort out the pissers.'

The whats? I followed him, but I wasn't sure that I'd be much use. The camp was full of people who seemed to know exactly what they were doing. They used words like 'pissers', 'photovoltaic' and 'consensus', and while I had an inkling what each of these terms might mean, I had no idea how I could help to sort anything out. Carrying hay, though, seemed a fairly easy thing to do, so I nodded and followed him.

'First time on camp?'

'Yup.'

'How are you liking it?'

'Well I only got here a couple of hours ago, but it seems good. Somehow...pure.'

'Oh yup, it's the ideal all right. Except for the planes overhead. Last year we were at Drax (another word that I didn't quite understand). It was beautiful there – middle of the countryside – pure bliss – except for the whopping great power station of course.'

So that was what Drax was. I wanted to take a little bow for having worked it out. It's the biggest coal-fired power station in Europe and the site of the first ever Climate Camp. I smiled and nodded as though I had known this all along.

'Right, first we've got to remove the soaked bales.'

We'd arrived in front of the compost toilets. I still felt none the wiser, but as I looked at the doors I noticed that some were labelled 'pissers' and others 'shitters'. So this is what I was expected to do... John handed me a pair of industrial rubber gloves, his own hands already shrink-wrapped.

'We need to take this bale out, wheel it over there, break it down and then put a fresh bale in. There are only three that need doing so it shouldn't take long.'

I smiled and wished that I hadn't been so determined to be helpful. This might have been John's utopia but it certainly wasn't mine. In my imaginary paradise, the water that I flush down my loo would not be a fifth of the water I use every day, but if that means compost toilets I don't want to be the girl in charge of them. John seemed to notice my dismay, quietly smirking to himself, but it was only my second hour on camp and I wasn't going to lose my cool. I pulled on the gloves and squared up to the pisser.

It was hard work moving the bales, and I soon had my jacket off as well, understanding now how he stayed so warm. Fifteen minutes of trying not to breathe through my nose later and the job was done! I had made my first contribution to the running of the camp, and hoped this would exempt me from being on toilet duty again. John began walking away, and I asked him where he was off to.

'There's a meeting in my neighbourhood. I'm facilitating.'

I bit the bullet. If I kept ignoring words that I didn't understand I was going to get very lost in conversations.

'What's that?'

'What?'

'Facilitating?'

He glanced me over, smiled and started to explain, as we walked together to the 'South Coast' section of the camp.

'We hold our meetings by consensus…'

I looked at him, confused.

'…which means that every single person in a meeting can contribute to it. So we usually hold meetings as neighbourhoods – there's London, which is huge and a bitch to facilitate; Scotland, the North-East, Yorkshire: quite a few, really. At those meetings we might discuss what tasks need doing and how we're going to be sure we get them done. But sometimes we have more serious issues to discuss, like – "Do we want media on site?" or "How will we liaise with the police?" – when we have those discussions in a neighbourhood, we'll try and come up with some proposals which then go back to the whole camp. So we all get to have our say on how the camp's run, all the proposals get heard, and finally we get consensus on what to do.

Everyone's part of making decisions, and everyone helps decide how the camp is run.'

'And that works?!'

'Uhmm, yes, well…slowly. It definitely works when it's camp things that we can take our time over. But it breaks when we need an immediate response. So if the police send out a press release saying that weapons have been found here then we need to send out a press release really fast to counter it. It would be crazy to get the whole camp to do that, so instead we have working groups who can make those decisions for us. Anyone can be trained and become part of a working group – if you're interested in the media, you join the media working group, and then you go to smaller consensus meetings, where people who can be bothered with the press write press releases and keep sending them out.'

'I think that's where I want to go: the media working group.' I liked the way this sounded, precise and efficient. Maybe in this area of the camp my past three years studying English would be of some practical use.

'They've got a training session tomorrow at two in the media tent. Go along, get trained up and get involved. Easy as that.'

He disappeared into the South Coast tent and I found myself alone again. Around me, everyone seemed pretty busy. The last time I'd camped was at a festival the year before, and amongst all these tents I had been aware of a familiar sense of excitement and anticipation

– but that was where the comparison ended.

Instead of sitting around with a can of beer in one hand and a fag in the other, talking to their friends about the band they'd just seen, everyone here was moving around, looking for something that needed to be done, calling a group together and then getting the thing done. What was weird was that somehow, whether they were changing the pisser's hay bales or chopping vegetables for hours, the people here seemed to be having more fun than the crowd at any festival I've ever been to. We'd come to Heathrow to create something different.

I was at the camp because, in my last week at university, two of my friends had ordered me to go. They'd lent me some climate science to get me good and scared about the impending apocalypse, and told me what building a third runway at Heathrow would mean for the climate.

My friends' scare tactics had done the trick and here I was. But neither of them had yet arrived, and a third friend, Jen, a first-timer like me, wasn't coming till much later that evening. I wandered back to the London Neighbourhood. We had the biggest tent in the camp, which wasn't surprising, as we were expecting thousands of curious Londoners to come and visit it over the week. I sat in a tent full of strangers, feeling less than sociable and wishing Jen would arrive. I was worried that people would work out that I was a phony, that I was only just getting serious about climate change and I didn't know

very much about it at all. It felt like the first day of school. I felt that
if Jen had been there, a friend to share this strange new place with,
then things would have felt so much easier. But as it was I had no
idea who was on a similar journey to me, and who was a climate
activist old-timer.

I was sat on the outskirts of a conversation. The exchange was
between a woman with white-grey hair in an incongruously smart
jacket, a girl about my age with a big smile who said she'd just
come down from Leeds and a bearded, fifty-something man, with
dark hair that tailed off in a single dreadlock. The girl mentioned
a phone call she'd had from her Mum, worried sick after reading
news reports that the camp was full of terrorists. The lone-dreaded
man gave a tight laugh.

'Same old media bullshit. We get it every year, throughout the
year. They're not interested in reporting what we're doing here. All
they want is a story that sells, where we seem like the bad guys. They
miss the issue every time. "The world is ending." Can't make news
bigger than that. But all that gets written is "Anarchists threaten
to…" or "Eco-terror rocks Heathrow". We shouldn't even be talking
to the media. They're not interested in what we have to say. They
just see what they expect to see and write a loada shite.'

He looked around with a bitter triumph, as if he expected the
other two to applaud him. I waited to see what the others had to say.
The older woman was frowning a little as she brushed a fleck of mud

off her jacket. Then the girl spoke up.

'Yeah...but I don't think that they can keep reporting the way they have for the past however-many years. Because things are changing so fast now. The media's got to stay on top of it all. Like, even George Bush has admitted that climate change is a man-made problem and the scientists are up and screaming about it all the time, and government advisors, and every charity – and now even I'm here, which just wouldn't have happened a couple of years ago. If the public know about climate change and they know that we're here trying to prevent it and they get to see the society that we create within this camp, then how can they see us as anything but heroes?'

I'd read the papers that morning. The coverage of Climate Camp hadn't been particularly positive. The headlines screamed: 'MILITANTS WILL HIT HEATHROW'. I had almost been convinced to undo my rucksack, put my tent away and watch the week from the safety of my living room. It was nice to think that the message of the camp, its peaceful, educational ethos, could have penetrated the media, but everything I'd read had been about the threat to security of having activists near an airport as important as Heathrow.

'Heroes?!' the man gasped. 'People don't see us as heroes. Typical ridiculous naivety. We're the enemies. We're the people who want to ruin your holiday, ground your flight, make your life hell. We're joyless prigs with nothing better to do than protest. It doesn't matter whether it's the most important protest there's ever been. What matters is that we're crazy hippies and that the public at large don't have a clue why we're here, so the media don't bother to explain it to them.'

'No, but it is changing.' She gave him a disarming smile and hugged her knees to her chest. 'A year ago I'd never have thought I'd be spending part of this summer camped outside an airport. A year ago I was on my way to Magaluf! But now I've read the climate stuff, I'm really scared and I'm trying to do something about it. Everyone I've met here has a different story. We don't fall into a stereotype. The media can see that.'

The grey-white-haired lady spoke. 'But they can't see it because we don't let them come onto the camp. We've only got ourselves and our handling of the media to blame. The press would probably love a story about a sixty-year-old resident of Twickenham, a grandmother of eight, getting out her tent for the first time in twenty years and joining a climate protest. But instead they're led round the camp by one person for a couple of hours a day and they don't understand our reasons for being here.'

The one-dreaded man stood up and lobbed his used teabag into the compost bin. 'What, and you'd rather have them crawling around the camp, watching us cook and eat and make fires and run workshops and set up wind-turbines and piss? We're not a zoo!'

'A zoo? We're not animals! The whole point is to talk to them.' The older woman looked at the younger one. 'She can tell them about climate change. You can tell them how long the government's known about the problem and how little they've done about it. I can tell them about Heathrow, the property prices and the pollution around my grandchildren's school. They could choose what they thought their readers would like to read. Then the anarchist stories would go away.'

There were clearly some differences of opinion, and a much bigger diversity of ideas than the media could ever show. The man, Tim, had been doing this sort of thing for most of his life. A protest camp was precisely where you would expect to find him. He'd only ever seen his good intentions misrepresented by newspapers that don't want to make their readers feel uncomfortable: 'Don't worry, it's just men like him who would ever go to a protest, you don't need to worry that anything's wrong.'

The younger girl's attitude was more unexpected. I wondered if she was like me and looking for a form of protest that might actually work. I wondered if she'd gone on that march as a teenager as well, the one where a million people said 'Not in my name!' and then Britain followed the USA and invaded Iraq anyway. Besides all the other fall-out of the war, back home we all lost faith in the march as a method of protest. We wanted to take a different sort of action, one that would ensure that climate change couldn't be ignored or treated as a political game.

The older lady was the most out of place, and it was true that her presence would have given the news reports a different quality. With her smart jacket and well-coiffed hair I could almost see the profile piece in *The Reader's Digest*. I wondered what sort of actions she'd taken before coming to the camp. Had she written to her MP? Joined Friends of the Earth? Given petitions to Downing Street? I thought about her grandchildren growing up under the flight path, with the deafeningly loud planes passing overhead every ninety seconds. She stood up to leave, wincing as she stretched her knees. I wondered how much discomfort she'd be willing to put up with to show the world how serious she was.

I shifted myself on my cushion and the girl from Leeds caught my eye and smiled. I smiled back shyly, but felt too full to talk. It was like I was pinned between these two huge, opposing forces. There was the overwhelming fear for the future, impossible to pin down. Then there was the even bigger hope that nothing in the future is fixed. What if this crisis was the most amazing opportunity to create a new sort of society, one where happiness wasn't measured in how many gigs you can fit on your iPhone or how big and exciting your wardrobe was? I'd only been at the camp a few hours, but already I was starting to sense that a different world might be possible. I'd grown up as part of the generation that had everything, but perhaps there had always been something missing – something about community, creating things together.

The sky had clouded over and started to spit with rain, and

gradually the London Neighbourhood tent filled up. People sat around reading leaflets and sharing books. The conversations around me ranged from in-depth discussions about carbon emissions to joke plans to steal one of the mounted policemen's horses and do some dressage through the camp. On one side of the marquee a large strip of white cloth had been unravelled and people were painstakingly hand painting the words 'Make Planes History.' I finally worked out how to be useful and started collecting dirty cups to be washed. Some diehards outside continued to hammer-in tent pegs and haul bales of hay in the rain. Suddenly, a shout rose above the afternoon lull.

Another voice yelled in response, and then another, until the quiet of the camp was broken by busy, panicked shouts. In the Neighbourhood tent everyone dropped what they were doing, left the marquee and ran in a long wave in the direction of the loudest cries. Together we leapt over tents and guy ropes, sprinting to the main gate of the camp where there was already a crush of people. We could see the rows of riot police and police vans behind them. Nearer to us was a line of activists, their arms held high. Behind them was a mass of people, more arriving by the second. Some pulled on anoraks as they approached. Others craned their necks and peered out into the line of the riot police. All I could see were the policemen's eyes. Their faces were masked with black balaclavas, which were covered by helmets with visors.

'Typical,' I heard someone mutter, 'as soon as the media have gone home, they start clearing us up.'

The idea of being 'cleared up' by this faceless arm of the law was terrifying. They were uniform. A clear shield on one arm which jabbed out if a protester got too close, the other hand fingering the baton, nervous and twitching and always ready to go. With our hands up, demonstrating our lack of weapons and our vulnerability to their blows, we assumed a peaceful stance. But there was massive tension in the air: no-one knew what the police were hoping to achieve, or how long we would need to stand defending our right to camp.

A man had his three-year-old child tied to his chest. He kept his eye closely on the police line in front as his little girl giggled and wiped the rain from her face. Suddenly the police charged.

The mass of people became an ordered, deep-ranked line of protesters with hands held up like kids playing cowboys and Indians, pushing the police back with the physical weight of their bodies and nothing more. They met our resistance with aggressive blows and snarled shouts.

'FUCKING MOVE!' One man was dragged from the lines of protesters, taken behind the lines of police and beaten hard. A roar went up: 'SHAME ON YOU! SHAME ON YOU!' Again we surged forward, our hands in the air, giving the police nothing but our bodies to storm against. For a moment the police held firm. Then we surged and they edged back. The gridlock of yellow uniforms, riot shields and helmets began to break down as the Climate Campers refused to turn and run, refused to be intimidated. Twenty minutes passed, and more protesters were pulled away from their friends, tugged beyond the police lines and beaten. We stood together and walked slowly forward. The police were pushed from the camp.

As the last of the riot police left our site by the main gate, we were buzzing with a new energy and a new sense of community. Groups form around a common purpose, but what binds them together is the opposition they meet. I had thought I had little in common with many of the people there, but when we found ourselves under attack we found that to the police, at least, we were completely indistinguishable. We were united by the police's treatment of us, and united in indignation that the people who were supposed to protect our safety had charged in and attacked us when we resisted. There was a buzz throughout the camp. The police had not been allowed to disperse us. We had stood together and we had pushed them out.

***

The next day, I woke up at 5am to the deafening noise of the first flights leaving Heathrow. I was at the camp because I was terrified of climate change, but the longer I stayed, the more of a local issue I realised airport expansion was. I couldn't imagine having to put up with this roar, ripping through the air every ninety seconds, throughout every day and most of every night. The police had lit a strip-light in the night, which had not yet realised that it was dawn. It shone relentlessly on. Bringing food in from the village, we were stopped and searched eight times: three times on the way out and five times as we made our way back with our supplies. I was laden with crates of bread. A boy carried two sacks of porridge and two others pulled a cart filled with veg. My arms aching, I was beginning to feel very much part of a unit, defined in opposition to the uniformed police. The frustration made me start feeling radical!

Mid-morning, I left the camp to go to the local charity shop, who I'd heard were doing great business in second-hand Wellington boots. The three ladies behind the till wanted to talk to me about the camp. 'I've heard that it's lovely down there.'

'Yup, yes it really is. We're just getting on with it, there are lots of workshops to learn about climate change, or how to mend a bike, or how to insulate your home – it's really, really incredible.'

They smiled and caught each other's eyes. I beamed at them. Maybe the camp wasn't their cup of tea but they were pleased, if a bit bemused, that it was happening.

'It's lovely to think that all these people might come back if they send bulldozers for Sipson.'

'Yup, we definitely will. You can count on it.'

I left feeling like a bit of a hero and went to the chemist to buy contact lens solution. Behind this counter, there was a different vibe.

'You one of them campers then?'

'Yes, that's right.'

'I think it's terrible, they come here, squat a field and sit around smoking drugs, drinking, littering…it's horrible.'

'We're stopped and searched by the police at least twice before entering the camp. I promise you, there are no drugs on site.'

I left deflated. We were neither heroes nor criminals. We were just a bunch of scared people, doing something we could only hope would work.

The media workshop that afternoon was run by a woman who clearly knew her strategy. A real pro, she could answer any of the questions that we threw her way, and I felt a bit inadequate. I knew that climate change was an urgent threat. I knew that expanding Heathrow would make it the UK's single biggest emitter of CO_2. I knew that the government wasn't protecting my future. But when I was put in the hot-seat and asked to explain why the camp had come to Heathrow I fluffed my lines and came across confused. We role-played an interview.

'Don't you think that you're just alienating people by breaking the law?'

'Well some people might feel alienated but maybe others will, uhmm…' I looked around me, feeling stupid. 'Are we even breaking the law?'

It turned out my confusion was understandable. We were dealing with some complicated legal issues. The camp was 'unlawful', but not criminal. We couldn't be arrested for going, though we could be stopped and searched just for being there. If we'd been planning to stay for longer the council might have got a court order to evict us, but that would still have given us twenty-eight days on the site. These are the laws that protect travellers and squatters, and are often used by protest camps to reclaim land. The police could clear us off, on the other hand, if they thought that criminal activities were being planned on the site. That was the justification they would have used if they'd managed to 'clear us up' the day before. But they could still only use reasonable force, and with a peaceful camp of people who refused to fight them that wasn't much. That's why non-violent direct action could be so effective.

I went back to my tent thinking about this term I kept hearing: 'direct action'. It seemed to mean a lot of things. Someone had given me a leaflet about its history, and I took it out and started reading. The stories were impressive. In America the Civil Rights movement boycotted services that had segregation. For over a year, 40,000 African-Americans in Montgomery, Alabama, didn't use the bus. Eventually, the law was changed and buses no longer had separate sections for white and black people. Mahatma Ghandi's most famous criminal act was simply making salt. The British had made it illegal for Indians to make their own salt, forcing them to buy it from British-owned companies. Ghandi walked 240 miles to the sea, gathering a huge group of people as he went – by the time they arrived the procession was two miles long – and then he broke the law openly, was arrested and put in prison. By the end of the month hundreds of thousands of Indians had also broken the law. It took another seventeen years before India won its independence, but its people acting en masse against the authorities was an integral part of their success.

Laws do change and societies change too. Ghandi was a lawyer. He tried to work inside the system, to win the approval of the British authorities and to fight for Indian rights through the courts. But when that didn't work he changed his methods. Rather than ask someone else to change the law, he just broke it and accepted the consequences. He wanted to change the hearts and minds of the British, but also of other Indians, to show them that they had the power to 'be the change'. He spent years of his life in prison, undertook hunger-strikes for weeks and suffered ill-health and hardship. His cause and message became famous throughout India and the rest of the world.

And what about us? Fighting for action on climate change is different to fighting for civil rights or independence. It's harder to identify the laws that need changing or the companies that need boycotting and in the West, at least, it can be harder to identify the people that will be sympathetic because at the moment we all benefit from using so much of the world's resources. But, on the other hand, we can be certain that change is coming, whether we like it or not.

RUSH!

I thought about the camp. It was a form of direct action just coming here and setting it up. We were showing the wider community that living sustainably – hay-bale toilets and all – was possible, and that we were already willing to do it. But we couldn't show the rest of the world what we had achieved if the only stories in the media were about eco-terrorists grounding flights. We needed more media attention, but the right sort of attention. Breaking the law and getting arrested would be one way of getting our message across, but we'd have to be careful about which laws we broke so that we weren't branded as criminals and the message didn't get lost.

As I sat and thought, staring absent-mindedly at the picture of Martin Luther King, I heard a voice in the tent next to me. Someone was talking into their phone, explaining what he thought of the camp and listening to the person on the other end. He must have been a journalist who'd come into the camp pretending to be a protester. He was grumbling about the vegan food. He missed his bacon buttie breakfast. (I hadn't been able to resist buying a sausage roll when I was in the village that morning. It's a weakness I have.) And now he was complaining about the police strip-light keeping him awake at night. So much for keeping the journalists off site.

Later that afternoon, I joined the row of campers cutting vegetables in preparation for dinner. Everyone seemed to know each other, smiling and laughing and teasing. They included me in their jokes. They taught me the words to a song. Soon we were all chopping in

60

unison, singing a 'call and response' melody, turning it into a round. The sun was shining through a slit in the tent's canvas. The world felt so right, the campsite almost too idyllic to be true. Three hours later we began to serve the dinner we'd prepared. The queue wound around the tent and out into the sun. As we spooned dollops of rice and curry and salad onto people's plates they grinned at us in thanks.

I'd signed up for gate duty that night. The camp had four entrances, each of which needed to be watched at all times, in case the police tried to enter in riot gear again. If it looked like this was going to happen we were told to push down on the middle button of the walkie-talkie. 'This is Gate 2 to Gate 5, do you copy?' We had to release the button and wait for the tinny voice, and then quickly press it again: 'Police on site, I repeat, police on site at Gate 2.' Apparently then the cry would go up throughout the camp and we'd be joined by hundreds of sleepy campers. I felt very important and a bit like Tank Girl.

Three hours into my five hour gate-watch I was cold and more than a little bored. I had just let my head loll on my shoulder for a few minutes of sleep when the walkie-talkie rasped around my neck. 'Gate 2, do you want some coffee or tea? Or rum maybe? I'm heading over to keep you company.'

Crackling through the muddy handset was the voice that I'd been waiting for. Jen had arrived on the camp and her voice was the perfect pick-me-up just as I'd begun to slump. Her off-hand familiarity made me grin and I pretended that I wasn't surprised to hear her voice transmitted from the communications tent.

She soon appeared out of the darkness, her tired face a reflection of my own. As dawn broke five policemen came and stood at our gate. I reported this to Gate 5. Jen ran back to the camp to fill up her thermos flask and get some cake. We shared it with the newly-arrived cops who were there, I think, to watch us watching them.

At 6am, Jen and I were released from gate watch, and headed back to our tent, my Converse trainers getting soaked in the long grass. On our way back, we became the audience to a different ideological battle. A guy standing by the biggest fire on site, who had spent the week clasping an ever-replaceable can of Special Brew, had been disturbed from his drunken haze and was shouting at one of the more 'right-on' campers. With an unlit rollie balanced on his bottom lip and a broken lighter in his hand he told the clean-cut eco-protester to 'piss off'. Jen and I had affectionately named this man 'mister liability', trying our utmost to hold him back from policemen's batons and the media's cameras. In the end the camper was forced to shrug his shoulders and retreat. Jen and I giggled as we headed back to the COMMS (communications) tent to hand in our walkie-talkies.

Later that day I was taken aside by a friend. As I'd suspected, it was understood that the presence of the camp itself wasn't really enough to capture the media or get our concerns about aviation and climate change out to the public. The camp was definitely moderate. Thousands of people had come to take part, and most of them were not that willing to push the boundaries. However, those who did want to take that extra step were encouraged to find each other, form small groups and organise autonomous direct action. Although the negative press had focused on flight delays and ruined holidays, the real target was BAA, the British Airports' Authority, owners of seven airports across the country. I'd heard rumours about blockades involving hundreds of people, but the action my friend was hinting at would be something smaller and more covert – I couldn't even know the details until we'd left the camp. I felt a little nervous, but I trusted her and I was excited to have been asked to get involved. I gave her a little nod, grabbed my stuff, and met her back at a van, heart thumping but happy. Soon I'd be on my way out of the camp, heading to an airport. The plan? To shut it down.

CHAPTER THREE

'THIS IS HOW YOU DO ILLEGAL DIRECT ACTION'
BBC *Newsnight*

We jumped out of the back of a white van, which had pulled up in front of a small private jet airport outside London: Biggin Hill. The BBC had been following us in their people carrier. As they took out their camera we got on with the job. Bike locks and arm tubes were passed around. The bike locks were to attach people to the gates of the airport and the arm tubes would lock a line of people together on the floor in front. We hoped that this would make it impossible for the police to remove one person without dragging the rest along the ground. It was my first direct action and I didn't feel ready to 'lock-on'. Instead I was going to help the others, roll them cigarettes, feed them water and turn the pages of their books. I was to liaise with the police and talk to the press, but I didn't want to be on the frontline.

I was with eleven people, only one of whom I knew well. I was less than two months out of university and less than two hours from my first arrest. But I didn't know that yet. I thought that as I had a 'support' role, making things comfortable for the others, I would not be a target for arrest myself.

My friend sat herself in front of the gate and I slipped the bike lock round her neck. She smiled as I locked it shut. 'Rather you than me,' I muttered, bolting it, before running down the road to ditch the key down the drain. Another seven people had arranged themselves flat on their backs on the Tarmac, connected by fat yellow arm tubes. They'd need to get in a professional cutting team to release them. Job done. Airport locked down. The sun was shining and I was riding high.

The morning had begun at 6am in a two person pop-up tent, shared between five. Now, the initial rush – the tent-packing, the short drive and the race to lock the gate shut – had passed. The adrenaline that had been pumping round my body for the last twenty hours kept me soaring, but there was nothing else to do. I fished around in my pocket for the daily newspaper horoscope that I'd read the day before. This is what it said:

'SCORPIO

Mars is in ascendance and you're feeling on top of the world. Well, Scorpio, for once you're not wrong to believe in fate. As Jupiter mingles with the fire of Mars you confront a change of direction. You'd be a fool not to take it. Today is your day and, whether it's appreciated or not, now's the time to take your future back into your own two hands.'

It's difficult not to read too much into the perfect horoscope. It makes you forget that a twelfth of the population could also have read it, that day or the evening before. Sometimes you just need to believe that the world is trying to tell you that what you are doing not only feels right but *is* right. These moments, when the world seems to speak to you and you alone, are signs of an absurd self-interest that could lead you to a very lonely place. But they can also be the moments that help you believe that you too can achieve incredible things. They make you a part of a bigger picture and give you a sense of purpose. I still have a clipping of that horoscope. It's glued to my wall. Hugely delusional – I know.

A chauffeur arrived shortly after us. He was driving an enormous silver Mercedes and sporting a cap. As he approached the gates it seemed he might try and drive straight through. But no – he jumped out and began getting indignant. He was wearing a pink shirt and his face was soon turning a similar colour. He barked at the *Newsnight* crew, but they didn't say anything so he came to row with me instead. It was good practice. In a little while *Newsnight* would want to give me a similar grilling. I explained as calmly as possible that we were here to stop private jets from taking off. I talked about human rights and responsibilities. I reminded him that 300,000 people were already dying each year from diseases that had spread because of rising temperatures.

I finished my spiel and we looked blankly at one another. There was nothing more that I could say and I wanted to turn away and walk off. He couldn't understand why the hell I was doing what I was doing and I was similarly baffled by the life choices he had made. It wasn't about to turn nasty; he wasn't getting aggressive; but the exchange made me sad. His world had been interrupted by ours. We had made it impossible for him to do his job and the only answers I had for him were things he couldn't care less about. I bounced right off my high.

I sat down a little apart from the protest. I watched the faces of the people chained-up − people who were prepared to barricade an airport so that they could save the world from a few tonnes of CO_2. It was a drop in the ocean. We couldn't even begin to combat climate change until people like this chauffeur understood and supported the actions that we were taking. People would probably see pictures of this protest and think we were mad.

I fingered the horoscope again. It seemed a bit ridiculous to have read so much into it. One airport for private jets could be shut for three hours by a group of activists who were prepared to face arrest. I had no idea how many airports there were across the world, how many coal-fired power stations, oil-refineries, cars or energy-inefficient buildings. We needed so much more than these small pockets of radical activity. We needed the majority of the world's population to demand a greener world. It all seemed a little hopeless. I felt myself deflating.

The *Newsnight* crew, I was told, were getting bored. They'd spoken to the chauffeur, they'd waited for the police to show and now they wanted to interview a protester. I was sitting in front of the gates with ten braver people locked behind me, but the cameraman had a good angle and my movements weren't limited by locks. It became clear I was the one they were going to talk to most. I'd done my media training and I hoped I'd remember something worth transmitting across the UK. I wished I didn't feel so miserable.

As the cameraman set up I talked to the presenter, squatting on the ground in front of me. It wasn't Jeremy Paxman; I was sure this guy was just as tough but still, it was a relief not to be confronted by the most notorious interviewer on the BBC. The chat calmed my nerves a little. Then suddenly the cameraman was ready to roll and the presenter said:

'But why do you have to do it this way? Why do you have to cause so much disruption?'

I faltered. I was so well prepared for questions about aviation emissions and airport expansion plans that I'd forgotten to remind myself why we were protesting in this particular way. What could I say that would make the television audience sympathetic? I didn't want to pause too long but I didn't have a ready answer. It was difficult to think clearly with a camera in my face, when for the last ten minutes I'd privately been thinking there was no point in protesting at all. I gulped, opened my mouth and listened to what came out with surprise:

'I think that we wouldn't have so much publicity... Uhmm... It's like the Suffragette movement. A lot of people think that the Suffragettes damaged the Suffragist cause, but without direct action there just wouldn't have been the awareness or the publicity for it to get off the ground.'

My heart was thumping as the interviewer continued with his questions. My breathing was tight and my voice sounded strange and small. This was the first time I'd talked to the press. Instead of sticking with the message I'd learnt I had said something unexpected and unprepared. I don't remember spending any more than three hours of my school years studying the impact of the Suffragettes, but their legacy suddenly seemed so relevant. If anyone was going to teach us how society could be reshaped, it was the women who had changed Britain a hundred years ago.

***

A year and a half later, Ed Miliband, our Secretary of State for Energy and Climate Change, said something that really caught my attention:

'When you think about all the big historic movements, from the Suffragettes, to anti-apartheid, to sexual equality in the 1960s, all the big political movements had popular mobilization. Maybe it's an odd thing for someone in government to say, but I just think there's a real opportunity and a need here.'

We need to change people's hearts and minds, and we need to look to the past for the kinds of actions that really worked to effect change. We need courage and we need civil disobedience. Unjust laws which only protect the powerful need to be broken. We need a movement so huge it will eclipse the successes of the Suffragettes. Hundreds of thousands of people will rise and take radical direct action. Up until now, we've had to rely on small groups of people using attention-grabbing stunts to bring the issue into the public eye. Larger groups might be able to shut down carbon emitters and save us a few more minutes of sleep. But the movement as it stands is not enough. We don't have anything that can compare to the Suffragettes or the Civil Rights movement and the changes that we need are even more radical than votes for women or fighting racism. But since we can be certain that change is coming, we can also be certain that a movement like this is on its way; we just have to hope that it'll come soon enough to stop a climate catastrophe. For once, a politician seems to be talking sense. I wonder how he'll feel when this mass movement becomes a reality; when it becomes deeds not words.

***

Back at Biggin Hill Private Jet Airport the police had just turned up. It had taken them two hours to get there but soon there were twelve police cars and we were outnumbered three-to-one by officers. They asked how long we were planning to stay. A couple of them looked at the bike locks and arm tubes and left to get bolt cutters. Of course, I was already loose, and suddenly one of them was arresting me.

'You do not have to say anything but it may harm your defence if you do not now mention something which you later rely on in court. Anything you do say may be given in evidence. Do you understand?'

I looked at him, then at the others behind me, and back at the police officer. I was just a support role, right?

'Uhmm, what for?'

'Aggravated trespass.'

One last glance back at the others and I nodded. He took hold of my wrists and snapped handcuffs around them. I couldn't really object when I'd known all along that the people I'd come with were going to be arrested, but my head was reeling. I just wasn't prepared for this. His strong grip around my arm and the pinch of the cuffs induced a stab of fear.

Sat in the back of the police van, waiting for my friends to be cut from their self-imposed shackles, I tried to talk casually to the three policemen sitting opposite me. They met my nervous chatter with

71

steely silence. They had a lot on their plates. We weren't the only group to have left the camp the night before and autonomous actions were now taking place at airports across the UK. The environmental movement had found its targets and the police were busily trying to pre-empt and react to this form of law-breaking. They didn't want to hear why we thought it so important to draw attention to the third runway. They just wanted to finish the job, begin the paperwork and stop patrolling a peaceful protest camp.

But this was my first arrest and I was full of nerves so I talked and joked and tried to make myself feel at ease. Finally, Mike, another member of the group, came and joined me, also cuffed. I started chatting but he gave me a look which said that speaking in front of the cops was definitely not a good idea. I felt stupid for having acted like such an amateur and shut up. Five minutes later we had both been uncuffed and put in the cage at the back of the police van. The doors were shut behind us and we sat in the dark, whispering to each other and waiting to be taken somewhere else.

Another hour passed and still the van didn't move. By this point Mike was desperate to pee and our conversation about the action had turned into a discussion of ways to hold it in and calls to the police up front to let him go in a bush outside. Instead he was told that if he needed a piss he'd have to do it in the van, and if he did that then he'd be arrested for criminal damage too. Mike folded his legs with a pained expression: 'Please can we go really soon?'

Eventually the van started up and we were on our way. Mike's face broke into a grin of relief. He couldn't know that we were going to drive for an hour around the M25 back to Heathrow, so that we could be put in cells in a station local to the Climate Camp. Poor guy.

At the station the cuffs were put back on and we were marched inside. I could see the other protesters getting out of the other vans that were pulling up. We caught each other's eyes and smiled.

Mike rushed to the loo while the police checked my empty pockets. 'Do you want to call anyone?' they asked. This had already been organised. I called the guy on legal support who had the numbers of all our friends and families. The police took my belt and my shoes, because they had laces. They made me take off my cross, the one I've worn since I was a child, and my ex's ring.

Twenty minutes later, I found myself alone in a cell. We'd been separated out and there would be no more cautious glances or friendly nods. Instead there were four grey brick walls, a steel toilet and a ledge topped with a blue plastic mattress. I sat down and began to stare at the walls. Soon I was bored so I stood up and walked round the room. Still bored, I decided that maybe I needed the toilet. There was no paper so I pressed a buzzer and waited.

There was no reply. They'd taken my watch when they'd booked me in so I had no idea how much time had passed. I didn't want to seem impatient but now I definitely did need the loo and so I buzzed again. Five minutes later there was still no reply, so I did what you do in these situations: peed, shook and pulled up my pants. When I sat back down I felt lonely, sad and a little undignified. It had been fun to be part of a team, on a covert mission, full of excitement and trying to save the world. Alone in a cell my convictions began to falter.

I was still new to the environmental movement. I'd been ready to be arrested, in principle, but this had really taken me by surprise. How could I have known that when the door of the cell closes behind you, all your certainty disappears?

Before getting involved in environmental activism I'd spent one night in a cell. I was eighteen, newly licensed and over the limit; I'd been taking my best friend home from a party, gone too fast the wrong way down a one-way street, and collided with an oncoming vehicle. I'd totalled their car, my car and a third one parked on the street, and narrowly escaped killing us all. Trapped in the police cell, drunk and terrified, memories of the crash whirred round my head. A car alarm blaring. The strobe-like flash of the approaching ambulance. Faye with her head slumped on the dashboard, the window that she'd smashed with her head when I spun the wheel glinting in the orange street-light.

I'd been totally, stupidly reckless. Throughout the night I thought about what kind of person that made me. Was I an irresponsible, thoughtless, dangerous idiot? Definitely. What if I had killed someone? Would I have been a murderer? I couldn't work it out. I knew that it was only luck that had stopped the worst from happening. I had totally violated all the principles I believed in most: the importance of love, justice and care for other people.

I still believed in those principles. I knew that this second arrest was different, that I'd taken action because I believed in them, because private jets were about the most unnecessary and polluting form of transport on earth. I started running through the facts I'd learn about aviation while I was Climate Camp.

⌛ TIME BOMB: *Aviation*

Aviation is not the biggest emitter of carbon. In fact, it is responsible for less than 5% of global greenhouse emissions.

That's much less than livestock (22%) and much less than rice cultivation (18%). But there are still good reasons for activists to focus on flying:

- It's growing really fast and will contribute 15% of greenhouse gases worldwide each year by 2050.
- 75% of flights are leisure trips. This makes them a luxury compared to the need for fuel for the emergency services or electricity for hospitals.
- Nearly 50% of all flights in Europe are under 500km, about the distance from London to the Scottish border.

These could easily be replaced with trains.

- Air travel is nineteen times more polluting than train travel.
- The top ten most popular destinations from Heathrow include Paris, Amsterdam, Glasgow and Edinburgh.
- If Europe continues on current trends the EU's entire carbon budget will be taken up solely by aviation by 2040.
- In the UK, the average income of people taking flights from Stansted is £47,000. Cheap flights are taken by rich people.

It's hard to talk about flying without sounding like you're preaching. I've certainly taken more than my fair share of flights in my life. I don't really feel guilty because most of them were taken when I was a kid and you just think that your parents know what's good for you. But I'd feel so bad if I flew now, because it is so much more destructive than everything else and makes every other sacrifice you might have made in your life seem pointless.

The average British person has a carbon footprint of 11 tonnes of CO_2 for a whole year. One return flight to Australia produces nearly 7 tonnes. You can change all your light bulbs, unplug all your phone chargers, take all your appliances off standby and recycle religiously, and one flight will cancel all those savings out. It's not that flying is never justified, but if you're taking climate change seriously you have to be absolutely sure it's worth it because flying is the single most polluting thing that an individual can do.

I can't stop anyone flying. I can't even stop my parents from flying. But in a world where so many things are out of our control this is one personal decision that will actually make a difference.

I knew in my head that our protest had been justified. But the quiet of a cell is a very strange place, where the difference between right and wrong or good and bad dissolves. I started to question everything. Would direct action really achieve anything? Could I actually make a difference, or was I just being reckless? And what about my future?

I perched on my mattress, wired on adrenaline and unable to sleep. My contact lenses were drying out and still the police ignored the buzzer. My vision was becoming blurred and the walls loomed in. The light was too bright and only thing to look at was a curved silver box on the ceiling. I wondered if it was a CCTV camera. I glared at it and felt watched and ignored and pathetic and not at all brave. The shutter opened and a face appeared through a hatch in the door. I glanced up, stood and said hello.

'Dinner time.'

The guard passed steaming Styrofoam through the grate. I wasn't hungry but I took it anyway.

'How much longer until I'm interviewed?'

'Not long now.'

'Can I have some toilet roll please?'

'Of course. Sorry about that; I'll get some for you now,' he smiled.

Half an hour later he hadn't returned. I glared at the silver box again and out of boredom opened up the Styrofoam and forked cool 'vegetable lasagne' into my mouth. As I was eating two policewomen came in. Now they wanted the rest of my clothes as evidence, though they couldn't tell me why. I was left alone with one of them as I changed into the white tracksuit they gave me. She didn't seem much older than me, and when she smiled at me there was genuine warmth.

'What was your protest about?'

It was such a relief to have someone to talk to that I just started blabbering.

'Well, uhmm, did you know that if Heathrow's third runway is built and we actually stick to our carbon emission cuts then by 2030 it'll be using all of them, I mean not leaving anything for heating and lighting, I mean that's just really insane isn't it?'

She nodded slowly. 'But is it worth, you know, giving your life for?'

'Of course it is!' I said, thinking of the city job I didn't go for, the parish life I would give up, the trips three times a year to Prague. 'If we don't do something soon, like now, like in the next couple of years, we're signing a collective suicide pact. We've got to fight it or we'll be in total despair.'

She gave me a startled look, and then the sergeant came back and took my clothes and I was alone again. I felt alert, on a high again. I had had a chance to talk about my beliefs and maybe, just maybe, I had cut through this young woman's scepticism and made her realise how serious the situation was. I might be all alone in here but the very fact that I'd been willing to get arrested would show people how much I meant what I said. That had to count for something, right?

A few minutes later and another officer opened the door.

'Come on, we're moving you.'

I didn't have anything except the clothes I was wearing so I followed him down the corridor. He showed me into an identical cell, only this one had 'THIS CELL IS UNDER 24 HOUR CCTV SURVEILLANCE' on the ceiling. I looked at him in confusion, and he gave me a grim smile.

'You're on suicide watch.'

The door clanged shut. I stood there, not really sure what was going on, until the door was reopened by the female sergeant.

'What's this about a suicide pact?'

I looked at her blankly.

'What?'

'PC James said when you were alone with her you started talking about a suicide pact.'

I guessed PC James was the younger policewoman. I mentally ran through the conversation I'd just had. The realisation dawned. She had completely and utterly misunderstood me. 'Uhmm I just meant that we're all going to destroy ourselves. Because of climate change.'

'Right...' she said, 'and you're not having any suicidal thoughts or feelings?'

'No, no. I'm just worried about climate change.'

The door closed again and this time I went and tried to listen to what was going on outside. I heard the younger officer say, 'But she said she wanted to kill herself...' I burst out laughing. So much for getting my message out to the public.

Another sixty minutes passed. The buzz of human contact soon wore off, and now I really was under the camera it felt even more claustrophobic. Eventually the door opened again. I breathed a deep sigh of relief. I was led to an interview room, introduced to a detective and politely asked to sit down. I was nervous and felt a bit shaky, but in a legal briefing at Climate Camp I'd been taught what to do: answer 'No comment' to every question they ask. That way you make sure that everybody's interviews are the same – nobody will incriminate themselves, or anyone else, and nobody will find themselves charged with conspiracy. My interview lasted forty minutes. I was asked the same questions in different formulations. I answered, 'No comment'. I was asked irrelevant questions. I answered, 'No comment'. I was told that my friends, the people I had taken the action with, had all answered their questions and been allowed out on bail. I was told that if I didn't answer then I'd have to stay until the morning when I would be taken directly to court. I was shocked and confused and horrified that this might be true, but I still answered, 'No comment'. Eventually the interview came to an end and I was allowed back into my cell. I was almost as relieved to be going back as I had been when they'd let me out.

I felt deserted. I didn't know most of the people who I'd been arrested with – why on earth had I thought that I could trust them to watch my back? I fell asleep, achingly alone. I was woken up some hours later and taken to a sink to wash my face. Three of the people I had been arrested with stood there, dirty and dishevelled, like me. Relief flooded through me, followed by a twinge of shame that I'd ever believed the police's attempts to manipulate me.

Putting people in prison – even temporary imprisonment in a police cell – is about more than controlling where they can go. It's about making them feel isolated and unsupported so that they'll betray the bonds of trust made outside. I guess I'm lucky that I grew up going to my grandparents' camps. I've always known that sense of community, that we don't live life as separate individuals. But I was new to the environmental movement and that trust was still fragile. It was nearly broken through the endless questioning, the countless times the police told me that I'd been abandoned. I promised myself that they would never play me so easily again.

***

My next arrest made headlines.

I was suddenly awake, in a single bed shared between three, in a cheap hotel close to the Houses of Parliament. I rubbed my eyes and thought of my priest, probably sitting in the side-chapel saying the Morning Prayer, and the excuse I had told him to get out of work that day. It's not very Christian to lie to a vicar, but I hoped he'd forgive me. I had a sick-with-nerves feeling in the pit of my stomach so I pushed the window open and stuck my head out into the cool February air. I felt dizzy – the same light-headedness that you get two minutes before being thrust on a stage, or in the seconds after you've opened the door of a squat before you dissolve into music and darkness. As the alarm yelled and the room filled with waking bodies I looked out over London and hoped I'd made the right decision in coming here. I could see Big Ben, and, just to the right, the roof we were about to climb on.

Ten minutes later we were downstairs. The others went to grab a coffee from the hotel's breakfast room but I couldn't deal with the stale smell of boiled eggs so I mumbled past them and sat on the step outside. It was too late to back out now, though questions kept whirring round my head: what if we get stopped? How high is it up there? Will the media care? What if they shoot at us? I knew that was pretty over the top but it was hard to stop imagining the worst.

It was a relief when a hand was laid on my shoulder and it was time to stop thinking and start acting: a short bus journey and then into the Houses of Parliament.

At the security points as we entered the building the adrenaline kicked in. It was a feeling I was getting hooked on – when months of planning takes shape and you're suddenly doing something that pushes the boundaries of what you thought you were capable of. The security guys took a grainy photo of me and searched my bag; I smiled the whole time through my nerves. When I joined the others in the lobby I was grinning at how easy it had been.

We stopped to re-group and join up with our 'insider'. He was carrying a large bag which we knew contained the banners and two pairs of handcuffs – things we couldn't have got past security. He was going to help us out onto the roof, and he was the one with the most to lose if we were caught before we reached it – then all the focus would be on him rather than on the protest and its message. In St Stephen's Hall he checked his watch and stopped. The rest of us stood close together, trying to look inconspicuous with the large rucksacks. 'We just need to pause a minute,' he said. I shifted from foot to foot, wanting to get on with it. I looked at the time. We wanted to be on the roof by 10am. It was thirteen minutes to.

We were stood next to a statue of a soldier. Sensing the tension, our guide pointed out a hairline fracture across the base of the sword he carried. 'This is a nice bit of history. In 1909 a Suffragette chained herself around this statue, and for over two hours she explained to the lobby why they had to given women the vote. They had to cut the sword to remove her.'

He smiled at us encouragingly and I felt the connection between us and another law-breaker, a hundred years before. I thought about the number of people who'd passed the statue in that time and heard what the Suffragette had done. I wondered if the actions of the environmental movement would make their way into history the same way.

Our 'insider' gave a little nod of his head to show it was time to move on. The route was tightly planned, with a small time frame to move in. My heart was thumping hard as we made our way through the building, past police checkpoints, always half expecting a shout and a uniformed arm barring the way. No reflection, no panic, just one foot in front of the next, measured breathing, the absolute necessity of not getting stopped.

We made our way up a staircase, past paintings of royalty and politicians, and then into a lift, which we went up in complete silence. Finally we were in a deserted corridor on the top floor. We stopped by a fire-door. Our insider gave one last look around, pushed the bar and we slipped out onto the roof of the Palace of Westminster. The door closed behind us and now we were breaking the law. The tense anticipation became a sickening relief. We hadn't been caught. We would be able to hang the banners. Then came the other realisation. We could definitely be arrested for this, and there was no turning back.

As we walked up the gangway to the northern end of the House of Commons there was a panoramic view of London beneath us that I will never forget. Up ahead was the London Eye, the best thing that BAA has ever backed, glinting against the Thames as it made its slow revolution. I turned and looked up Whitehall, stretching down to Nelson, now only about five metres taller than us. Three of my friends climbed down a set of step-ladders to a lower level of the roof and began unfolding and tying the banners. The fifth guy and myself took out the handcuffs and attached ourselves to the railings. They were cheap ones from a sex shop, and when I gave them a tug to test that they were firmly attached they broke.

'Er, Graham...'

He looked over and started laughing. I closed my hand round the broken metal and hoped no-one would notice. Once the banners beneath us were secure they dropped them both with a satisfying '*whoompf*!'. The air bristled against my skin and a smile danced across my lips. We'd done it! The House of Commons was now branded, for everyone to see: 'BAA HQ and NO THIRD RUNWAY.'

Later, when our distant figures appeared on the BBC, the interviewer only wanted to ask us questions about our supposed breach of security. 'It's nothing,' I stuttered, frantically trying to steer the conversation to the real issues, with background noise buzzing in my headpiece, 'to the security risk…that the government is taking, by allowing BAA to write part of their consultation paper on the third runway.'

'Right,' says the BBC journalist, 'I mean I fully understand that you want to point out why you are there – I think the security issue is of considerable concern to quite a lot of people as well…' There was a hint of laughter in his voice which made me uncomfortable. Then the interview was interrupted because the feedback was so loud.

Eventually I was allowed to make my point. 'Over 70% of Londoners don't want a third runway, yet BAA are allowed to write up parts of the document which the government are consulting over.'

The journalist prodded me. 'When you say "write up"… They have obviously been a party to the process, because they run the airport – as well as six other British airports.'

I realised, suddenly, how this worked. He wasn't really challenging me, just trying to get me to be more specific. 'But they've been taking a greater part than that.' I emphasized. 'Greenpeace has uncovered documents from the Department for Transport that show that BAA has been tampering with the data in the consultation report. They've been pushing through their agenda from the beginning, with the full support of the government.' I was finding it hard to find the right words. I made a face at one of my fellow protesters in embarrassment.

'Can you just wave for us?' said my interviewer, 'I think we can see you clearly in our shot now.'

An hour later, we were still on the roof. Members of the security team had joined us on the gangway, but the passage was so narrow that they couldn't remove us without our co-operation, or even approach us if we didn't let them. The 'powers-that-be' may have a lot of advantages on their side, but the restrictions of health and safety rules can tie them in knots. One security guard tried to get past me to get down the stepladder and I put up my free hand.

'You're pushing me. It's not safe. Get back.'

He looked at me, weighing up the situation. An accident was unlikely, but if I slipped and hurt myself when he was anywhere near me the House would have a million-pound-law-suit on its hands. Also, as we would have to come down at some point anyway, there was no real point in rushing the operation. He gave me an annoyed look and took a few steps back down the gangway.

Another hour passed. I kept the broken metal of the handcuffs firmly pressed to my palm so they'd still think they needed a professional cutting team to come in and release me. We'd taken countless calls from the media, and now we just had to wait for Gordon Brown to enter the House. Once he'd driven into the courtyard below us we'd give ourselves up for arrest and join the waiting police. But he didn't drive that day. Instead we were told that he'd delayed Prime

Minister's Questions and would use a side-door to enter. It seemed strange that he would take such lengths to avoid our protest.

Later, during the House's debate, he trumpeted: 'Decisions will be made in the chambers of this House and not on its roof.' Twelve months later Gordon Brown gave permission for BAA to build a third runway at Heathrow Airport without allowing the House to vote on it. It seems that the decisions about airport expansion aren't made on the roofs of Parliament or in its chambers. Our banner wasn't too far off the mark when we labelled the House of Commons 'BAA HQ'.

Gordon Brown refusing to provide our challenge with an audience made for a bit of an anti-climax. All we could do now was 'unlock' ourselves (I pretended I was getting out the key from my bra and fiddling with the handcuffs), come down and allow ourselves to be arrested. We were led out the way we came and found seven officers were waiting for us on the other side of the door. This time the constable decided we didn't need to be cuffed by them. We'd been polite throughout the protest and he trusted we'd stay that way. We were led through the Commons and out into the courtyard before being seated in a police van. We were pretty pleased with ourselves and our smiles were contagious. One policewoman laughed with us before slamming the van door and climbing into the front.

We were booked into the police station and were then left in our separate cells. This time I knew what to expect. Being separated from the others didn't mean that I was alone. The walls around me were just walls. I was one of five people who together decided to take direct action, who had found a great opportunity for transmitting a message, and who believed that the media would bite. Inside we couldn't be sure how much coverage our action had been given, but we could be sure that as a unit we'd done something we could be proud of.

Ten hours in, seclusion was becoming dull. Out of the silence the strains of an old protest song pierced the thick walls and metal door.

'And we are sitting for revolution; *Bella Ciao, Bella Ciao, Bella Ciao Ciao Ciao*. And we're in prison for revolution; I hope the revolution's now.'

I whistled back the refrain and an echoing whistle answered from a different direction. I grinned and starting clapping. We all began to whistle and the separate notes rang through the walls and met in the world outside.

I thought back to a time when I'd been arrested as part of a larger group. There'd been fourteen of us. Locked in my cell, I heard the words of a familiar song sung loud. After each line of the song, the singer was answered by five voices emerging from five separate cells. When the voice had run out of lines to sing a different voice began the call and response once more. When we fell silent the policemen knocked on our doors and asked us to start again.

When I was released the next day, I stepped into the waiting room of the police station and was immediately surrounded by friends. It was such a relief to see them, the people who had waited all those hours so that we could come out to friendly faces. Quickly, though, they told me to keep away from the door. There were photographers outside demanding a shot of the newly released 'Commons Five'. It's not as difficult as you might think to capture media and public attention. You just need a really good photo and a strong, visible message.

A couple of my friends collected the papers afterwards. A lot of the articles focused on the security issue – What if we'd been terrorists? How did we get in? – but each made a brief mention of our cause. A couple of weeks later, I spotted a piece in *The Sun*. This newspaper isn't usually sympathetic to our concerns, but even they suggested that people pay attention to our message.

***

It's difficult to communicate something to people who don't seem to think like you, and it's hard to feel part of a community with people you don't really know and whose views you're not sure you understand. But there are times when things begin to click. I'd never felt like part of The Sun's million-strong readership before, but reading that article, just for a moment, it was talking my language.

Sometimes at protests there's the same feeling. At first you're standing next to someone you don't know, ignoring each other in that British way we have, and then suddenly you're a community, shouting the same slogans and grinning encouragement at one another. Out of all of the groups I belong to, the 'bike tribe' are the best at keeping their cool and their distance, but there was this one time where I really felt like a member of a community even with them. On the last Friday of every month there's an event, a bike ride through London, called 'Critical Mass'. Nobody organises it, and there's no planned route; it's just hundreds and hundreds of cyclists going through the city, stopping traffic, taking on the taxi drivers and watching out for each other.

We met at Waterloo and then headed down to Parliament Square. We circled it a few times and then went into town. At first I felt shy – it seemed like everyone else knew each other. I had a few friends around but it was easy to lose them as you adjusted your speed to keep the line of bikes even enough that the traffic didn't break through. Then I stopped to help block off one of the roads and started talking to one of the other cyclists. He told me he'd never seen a girl riding a bike in such a large skirt before and I laughed at his Lycra. Pretty soon he'd introduced me to his girlfriend and soon they were talking to my friend Chloe about nights-out in Bristol.

A few streets later I saw a taxi driver get out of his car, shouting at the girlfriend to move out of the way where she was protecting the rest of us. She stood there, impassive, trying not to wind him up. Another cab was trying to nose through at the same time. Without any sort of signal half a dozen people suddenly stopped and surrounded the cab, forcing it away from the bikes. An ambulance, siren wailing, was nudging its way through the gridlocked cars. As soon as it reached the road we'd blocked off it set off past the cyclists, who all pulled quickly to the side. It moved a lot faster than most of the emergency services do at rush hour.

Later, I got chatting to a guy called Mark. He was an anarchist from Glasgow and was a hardcore cyclist. We circled the Barbican roundabout together, talking about the environment, politics, animal rights and activism. He gave me a DVD and an invite to an anarchist conference in a squat, though I had another meeting to get to and had to turn him down. I left the crowd in London Bridge, doing a U-turn and cycling back past the tail end. I *whooped* and a chorus *whooped* back at me.

As I cycled back through London I forgot that cyclists don't usually talk to each other. At the traffic lights I turned and smiled at the guy pulled up next to me. He looked at what I was wearing with an amused grin. I gave him a flyer and told him to come to the next action I was organising.

'Will you be wearing that?' He said.

I looked down at my large white skirt, frilly shirt, and red sash. I grinned at him. 'Yeah everybody will!'

The lights changed and I sped off, my white skirt billowing, proud to be a Climate Suffragette.

⌛ TIME BOMB: *Women and Climate Change*

The Suffragettes played a huge part in creating the world I grew up in – a world where being a woman didn't seem to be a disadvantage at all. Apparently the fight was over. There was no need to throw ourselves under horses, starve ourselves in prison, burn our bras or use words like 'sisterhood'. In fact, those things seemed kind of embarrassing. We had the vote, equal pay and the pill. Feminism had won – so why keep shouting about it?

But the more I learn about climate change the more of an illusion this seems. Climate change affects poor people and 70% of the world's poor are women. 75% of environmental refugees are women. 85% of the victims of climate-induced disasters are women. Across the world, women still don't have access to basic education and healthcare, and those disadvantages make them especially vulnerable to climate change. If millions of women around the world are suffering in this way, then thinking that feminism has won because a small number of us have made the Fortune 500 is like thinking that women in Elizabethan times must have had it real good because their ruler, Queen Elizabeth, was a woman.

Back home in the West, where we apparently have everything, women are suffering from the commercialized version of femininity we see every day – the one-size-fits-all, porn star aesthetic that stares out from plastic surgery ads along tube platforms and the gym ads that make women look fat by dressing them in jeans two sizes too small. In 2006, five times as many American women had breast enhancements than during the year before. Teenage girls have seen a huge rise in mental health problems. Half of my friends at school had eating disorders – and under-eating is really the same problem as overeating. It's about not trusting yourself to know your limits in a world that is relentlessly telling you to consume. The parcelling up and selling of more and more of the world's resources – right down to our own bodies – is causing catastrophic climate change and making women all over the world incredibly unhappy.

But there is cause for hope. For whatever reason, western women seem to care more about climate change than western men. In countries where there are more women in government they pass more legislation to protect the environment. It's women who decide what clothes to buy, what food their families eat and who have most control over the household – which account for 30% of the EU's carbon emissions. I like to think that women are taking a lead on this: recognising the price we pay for uncontrolled consumerism, the need to fight for the rights of the victims of climate change and the power that each of us has to lead that change.

The Dalai Lama said recently that western women would change the world. I set out to find some real life examples of women putting their ideals into action, and I was truly inspired by what I found. Here are some of their stories...

Margot Bowman, twenty years old, is studying graphic design at Central St Martin's College of Art and Design and lives in Hackney, London.

At the moment my favourite thing in life is riding my bike. Cycling makes you very aware of the climate. Shops and the tube are artificial places but if you cycle, you ask yourself questions like 'Why is it raining so much in July?'

My other favourite thing has always been clothes. I used to buy a lot of them – mostly on impulse in high street shops like Primark or Topshop, on a Saturday to wear that night and probably never look at again. Cheap clothes are great when you're a teenager. You get to pretend to be a grown up with real disposable income and when you're fifteen that – and boys – is all you care about. It's a rush.

High street clothes shops are a bit rubbish though really, aren't they? They're too predictable; after a while, everything in them starts to seem the same. A couple of years ago, I started to buy vintage. Having just one of something makes it special. You're still buying into a story but it's a better story.

It's a movie, not an advert.

As for other kinds of ethical shopping, my friends and I mostly go on instinct because we don't trust any of the stores themselves to be honest. I don't shop at Primark, however broke I am. Who knows where they really stand on sweatshops? That way of shopping is ugly because it feels ugly. It's the same when I see someone carrying a Louis Vuitton handbag. It makes me think: who are you? Are you saying that you're Louis Vuitton?

I still love fashion and still buy too much. Obviously, that isn't sustainable but for me, it's all about staying mentally aware instead of slipping into the fog. I'm trying to learn how consumerism works so that I'm in control of it – and not the other way around.

Tracey Howard is a youth worker. She lives in Sipson, Essex, one of the villages threatened by the third runway at Heathrow. She has two children, aged nine and fifteen. When the announcement was made that the third runway was going ahead, I was in the King William IV, the pub I work in part-time, and it was such a heart crashing moment that I had to go and recover in the loo with the landlady. I thought, well, that's it, I've got nothing to else to lose now. If the runway is built, I lose my home, my job, my kids' schools, even the place where my husband's grandma is buried. It was very poignant.

When the dust settled, we began to work out what we were going to do. There was definitely a blitz spirit, a sense of everyone coming together. We had memorabilia evenings with the older members of the community, asking them to bring down photos from when they were children. It was as if the village had been living in limbo for a long time, not knowing what to do, but from that moment everyone had a focus.

Very few of us are in a position to move. I'm in a Housing Association house, so I go wherever my Housing Association puts me. For the private owners, BAA [the British Aviation Authority, which owns Heathrow] had issued bonds, promising to pay 2002 prices, but then they said they didn't have the money. Since the announcement, the properties have become worthless.

I was crying but then we started planning. We realised that the best form of defence is attack. We're starting with flash mobs. Some are talking about cementing themselves to their houses. I'm a sitting tenant so I'll make use of squatters' rights. There's a local travelling community and they'll be invited to stay in people's gardens. Japanese knot weed will be planted – it eats concrete. If I have to get arrested, so be it.

It's a happy village, this one. Parents sit out in the close on benches and kids hopscotch next to the cars. Everyone knows everyone else's children's names and just going to the corner shop, you'll say good morning to twenty people or so. There are lots of cultures but no rows and I've never known a granny get mugged.

I know I'm blonde, but I've got big plans for the campaign and I intend to stay here. I want to bring my grandkids into this house.

Rebecca Sullivan, aged twenty-eight, runs Reap & Sow, a PR consultancy for sustainable businesses; Dirty Girl, a women's farming co-operative; and is president of her local WI group. She lives in the Cotswolds and is also studying for an MA at the Royal Agricultural College, Cirencester.

I grew up in south east Australia where there's no water – it was two-minute showers from day one – and it was rural so I knew where my food came from. I moved to London in 2001, where I started working in the wine industry and then was drawn into the slow food movement. From that I founded Reap & Sow, which advises sustainable businesses on how to raise their profile and improve their corporate and social responsibility.

Some women obsess about finding a man and having kids. My priorities are more about trying to save the world. I've just moved out to the Cotswolds after six years in London. I live on two acres of land, am digging a trout pond, putting in some hives and I grow all my own vegetables. This is where I run Dirty Girl Kitchen from.

Dirty Girl is all about encouraging women to go back to the land. By 2012, I'm planning to have set up between twenty and forty co-operatives all over the country. Members can grow potatoes in their gardens or strawberries in their window boxes, either as a hobby or commercially, but have the support of other business mentors to advise them. I just sold thirty jars of jam to a café in Bath.

When I tell people about the Dirty Girl concept, they think it's the best thing, so why is it the only one of it's kind? I've set up a network of mentors from all over the food industry because with women, striking out on your own is so much to do with confidence. It feels like a big risk. If men want to be farmers, they'll be farmers. I don't know too many women farmers.

People can't believe that I moved out here on my own. They always assume I must have moved to be with a man. Actually, I'm reconciled to the fact that I'll probably stay single. Of course part of me wants a family, but guys are a little intimidated by women who have this much ambition and drive.

And I'm thinking about choosing not to have kids. Do I really want to have children when we don't know if humanity is going to exist in fifty years time? If your great-grandmother was alive now she'd probably tell you not to have children – mine died last year at the age of a hundred and she was the number one person pushing my dreams of saving the world.

Isabel Adomakoh Young, aged sixteen, is co-author of the *Lionboy Trilogy*, *Lee Raven: Boy Thief* and *Halo* (forthcoming). She lives with her mum in Shepherd's Bush. I've lived in London all my life but I try not to be too 'city-fied'. Since I was really small I've been going to this wine farm in Italy. I love getting up at 7am and spending all day helping – you enter into this weird mindset looking at the plants and start to feel like each one is precious. There's so much freedom there.

This year we're going to take the train to Italy for the first time – it's a lot more hassle than flying but every time we do fly, it just feels so wrong. We're quite green otherwise: we grow our own food and don't really use a car.

I think people are very negative about teenagers, we've got this rep like 'I don't care', but there's always teenagers on protests and me and my friends do talk about the environment as well as *Big Brother*. But it's hard when you live in someone else's house. If teenagers had their own homes, they'd probably be a lot greener. Boys seem more into the politics and girls seem more into the ecology side.

In a way I'm hopeful about the future – there's so much

attention and pressure now. It's like everyone's been walking in one direction and someone at the back has been shouting 'Stop, you're going the wrong way!' Now everyone's stopped walking but they still need to turn round and come back.

I've got a sewing machine and I go to classes with my best friend to learn to make my own clothes. It's cheaper and you know for sure they haven't been made with slave labour. It's important to know that you can do things for yourself. I want to know that I'm prepared in case the worst happens. Like I always carry a lighter with me in case I get trapped somewhere and I keep scissors and glue in my bag. If it comes down to it, the farm in Italy is my place to run away to if the world floods.

Eugenie Harvey, aged forty, runs We Are What We Do and lives with her husband and seven-year-old old step-daughter.
I had some experiences when I was young which really affected me: my parents got divorced when I was about ten years old, our house burnt to the ground a couple of years later and I went from being a chubby kid to an obese teenager.

It gave me a keen sense of empathy that it took a few years to find expression for. After university, I got swept up in the media of the early 1990s – it was an exciting time with everything globalizing and technology exploding. I worked for a TV start-up of Rupert Murdoch's. Then I moved to London from my native Australia after ten years, looking for a change. Suddenly spending time on my own, I realised I was a long way from where I wanted to be – doing something important which could help others.

It was around the same time that I read about climate change. There was debate then – this was 2000 – but I'm a natural pessimist so I assumed it was a problem. Then I met David Robinson who runs a charity called Community Links. I asked him how ordinary people got involved with social and environmental issues and he said, 'Well, they don't. Certainly not as much as they did a generation ago'; and we started thinking of how we might get ordinary people involved.

I left the corporate world and we set up We Are What We Do with the aim of inspiring people to use everyday behaviour to make a positive difference. We're most famous for projects like the book *Change the World for a Fiver* and the 'I'm not a plastic bag' shopping bag. It was through my work that I met my husband, Andy Thornton, and my step-daughter. Now – well, I'm a living example of what happens when you grasp the nettle and do the thing that has been given to you to do.

There's no silver bullet that will solve climate change. Sometimes it's frustrating when you know that time is so short but I believe that you have to be realistic about where and how people lead their lives. Our job is to meet people where they are, not where we think they should be.

And I've got Cara to bring up. It's hard trying to explain to a seven-year-old why I don't like her going to McDonalds and coming home with endless plastic trinkets. But you've got to spend the time to find the words. Cara was born in 2000 and we know that anyone born in this century will feel the affects of climate change in their lifetime. We have a moral duty to try and reverse its effects and to educate the next generation. I don't want to have to explain to my children that I knew there was a catastrophe waiting for them in the future and I didn't do everything within my power to minimise the effects on them. No parent wants that.

CHAPTER FOUR

ST STEPHEN'S HALL STILL BEARS THE MARKS OF Marjory Humes's protest, back in 1909. She chained herself to that statue because she wanted to force those in Parliament to listen to her demands. She made herself a nuisance. She made herself a fixture. She made history. There is a plaque next to the statue celebrating her action, and her story is part of the tourists' guided tour.

Emmeline Pankhurst started the Women's Political and Social Union in 1903. She'd been involved in women's rights for years. She'd started off in the Women's Franchise League that won women the right to vote in local elections about ten years earlier. But the public were losing interest in the issue. By 1905 the media had stopped talking about women's rights. Letters and articles in support of them weren't getting published. Emmeline started thinking about other ways of getting attention. She was going to start making some noise.

In 1905 she broke in on a public meeting with a government minister, shouting, 'Will the Liberal government give votes to women?' over and over again. When she wouldn't shut up they brought in the police to drag her out. She kicked and struggled and spat in an officer's face. She was charged with assault, and when she refused to pay the 5 shilling fine she was put in prison.

In 1906 the *Daily Mail* coined the term 'The Suffragettes', to make a distinction between them and the more conservative Suffragists. The radicals knew a good brand when they saw it. At the height of their influence they could attract hundreds of thousands to their rallies. They had shops all over the country. A third of them went to prison for their beliefs. They would carry white arrows on marches as a sign of bravery. You can't help but be impressed with an organisation that inspires a thousand women to endure prison.

***

Hundreds of climate activists were converging on Manchester for a weekend of meetings and discussion about the next Climate Camp. The gatherings work a bit like the camp. A time and a place is decided, and the local group arranges space for meetings, meals, sleeping and entertainment. Over two days decisions are made, proposals are agreed on and we all return home with a strategy and a set of jobs to do.

I arrived on a coach from London. It was Saturday, I'd been out the night before and, unsurprisingly, I'd missed my nine o'clock ride. After four hours of staring out the window, feeling sick as a dog and wanting to scream at the kid behind me who kept kicking the back of my chair, I was in a foul mood. The coach pulled in, and as I threw my rucksack over my shoulders and picked up my sleeping bag my phone rang.

'Hey.'

'Hello, have you arrived?'

'Just got off the coach this second. Where do I go?'

It was Tali. We'd stayed in touch since I'd met her at my first Climate Camp. I'd chopped courgettes with her on my second day at Heathrow and she'd made me feel completely at ease. Most people know her as the one that stands to the front of the queue when meals are being served. She washes your hands as you pass. No doubt this is for the purposes of hygiene but you wouldn't know it by the way she touches you – there's nothing sterile about it. It lets you know that you've come to the right place, that you really do belong.

As she gave me directions I felt the frustration of the coach trip leave me. Soon I was smiling down the phone. I was on my way to the Climate Camp national gathering and it felt like coming home.

***

'I just want to do an experiment. To check the gender balance in this room.'

I didn't really see the point. It seemed an odd way to close a day of meetings. I was hungry and I could smell garlic bread cooking in the kitchen.

'Can you spread out in the room – those who think they speak a lot on the right, and those who think they don't contribute all that much on the left?'

I've always thought of myself as a confident speaker. Incidents like the 'myzled' episode never put me off for long. I placed myself as far as I could towards the right, and as I looked around the room I saw an even spread of men and women. It was good to know that we were all having our voices heard.

'OK, that's strange. Because the spread is fairly even...but I was noting down whether the people who spoke in that session were women or men, and the actual spread was sixteen women to eighty-one men.'

There was a moment of silence. I wondered if everyone else felt as shocked as me. Or maybe not shocked – it wasn't that dramatic, just a weird empty feeling, like that moment when you realise your bike's been nicked. I walked out of the room, left the community centre and went down to the river outside. I couldn't remember having said anything in that morning's meeting so I

RUSH!

sat and wondered why I hadn't. I took *Grazia* magazine out of
my bag and flicked through pages of celebrity gossip. The model
Lily Cole was staring up at me, on the arm of a male celebrity
who she may or may not have been dating. I remembered reading
somewhere that she supported Water Aid, and I wondered if this
sort of magazine would ever think that was interesting enough
to write about. Actress Emma Thompson was on the next page,
posing outside an awards ceremony. They thought her dress was
the wrong colour. Next page. Madonna. An article about how
amazing it was that she could still show her abs at fifty. A sex
object for three decades, hailed as a great role model for today's
young women.

I felt small and deluded. Everywhere I looked people were telling
women to dumb down, to be less than they might be, and now it
seemed the same problems existed within the camp, where I'd felt
so safe. It terrified me that try as I might to be a confident speaker
I was held back by something deeper, something I didn't even
know was there. It made me feel really, really sad. If I wouldn't
speak up, then who would?

Then I turned the page again and my eye fell on something
else. Like the horoscope I'd read before my first arrest, there was
a sudden clearing of the confusion. There, in an article about the
Edwardian dress revival, was a small piece about the Suffragettes.
The angle of the piece focused on their white dresses. White and

gold would be this summer's colours. But in amongst the fashionista text was a small, almost hidden fact, and a date that would come to define my life henceforth: October 13th 1908. On this day, as dusk fell, 60,000 Suffragettes had rallied in Parliament Square before rushing the House of Commons.

The centenary was about six weeks away.

That evening a buzz electrified my skin. Two months was just about enough time: just…if I started right now… I spent all night running over ideas in my head, high-tailed out of Manchester the following day, dashed to my church office and designed a flier for the 'Climate Rush'. The door of the office opened and Tom, the secular youth-worker, walked in.

If you're working in a church and something good happens it's tricky not to fall to the floor and thank the Lord. I just about stopped myself.

Tom was a local kid and found any indication that he was working in a church pretty hard to bear. How could he know his entrance was the answer to my prayers? I showed him my mock-up of a flier and asked whether he could put it online and create a Climate Rush website: www.climaterush.co.uk. In less than ten minutes, the Climate Rush went live: an idea, a printer churning out fliers and a website.

***

rush 1 (rsh) *(From www.thefreedictionary.com)*

v. rushed, rush·ing, rush es

v. intr

1. To move or act swiftly; hurry.

2. To make a sudden or swift attack or charge.

n.

1. A sudden forward motion.

2. Surging emotion: a rush of shame.

3. General haste or busyness.

4. A sudden attack; an onslaught.

***

So it was happening. There was no time to lose and I needed a lot of friendly support. The best thing about the environmental movement is that the community keeps your hopes high and motivates you. I picked up my phone and began calling my friends. When Jules picked up the phone I knew I had to be careful:

'So you're using the Suffragettes to rebrand the green movement?'

'Uhmm, not quite. It's more that I'm celebrating their actions and asking where that radical spirit has gone. I'm focusing on women, giving women a space where they can speak out and not feel bulldozed by men.'

'What do you mean you want to find the Suffragette's radical spirit?' She was indignant. 'God, Tamsin you're such a cock. There's radical feminism all over the place and a radical green movement too.'

'Yeah, I know, but it's not a mass movement. I mean, it's small. The politicians don't have anything to be scared of. No-one's holding them to account.'

'Oh right, and you're the girl that's going to change all that? You're going to conquer the political gridlock with a ferocious call to change? Women across the country will drop their copy of *Heat* magazine to stand beside you and fight for the right to fly less, buy less, be less? Good luck sweetheart, but this one looks like delusions of grandeur to me. You're not Emmeline Pankhurst. You're not even some second-rate Suffragette that history forgot. You're just a pretty face that looked good on the roof of Parliament and has let her "profile" run away with her.'

'OK, thanks Jules, sorry to bother you.'

I hung up, feeling crushed. There was probably some truth in what she said but something told me to trust my instincts. I really did believe that we could have more fun in a community of protesters rather than going out shopping or something. But with less than two months to go the project needed more than people just lending a hand: it needed a real flash of inspiration.

***

'Guess what! I've quit my job!' Lotti was bubbling over with excitement as she came into my brother's living room, where I was living temporarily. 'No more stupid HR woman bossing me about! I'm going to be a full-time campaigner!'

She 'high-fived' me and collapsed on the battered armchair. I'd made friends with Lotti through Plane Stupid. Her dream in life was to be a Greenpeace campaigner, but she knew you had to volunteer with them for about twelve years before you could get a paid job so she'd started doing some activism in the meantime. I grinned at her.

'Welcome to the club!'

I'd left the parish job, and my room in the vicarage, a week ago, and was now begging floor space off my brother while I worked on the Rush and tried to find a way to take my life in a new direction. We had both saved up enough cash to keep afloat for the time being, but knew that at some point we would have to lose at least two days of activism a week to temping in order to pay the rent.

Lotti curled up in the chair and looked at me.

'So what's this idea about a Climate Run?'

'It's a Rush not a Run,' I laughed.

'What's the difference?'

'I dunno really...that's what's so good about the word – no-one really knows what a Rush is, so it could be anything. Like when the Suffragettes held one I'm guessing half the people who wound up hammering on the door of Parliament didn't plan to break the law that day. They just turned up and then there was this feeling in the air.'

Lotti hooked up her hair and held it in place with a pencil. 'You've been watching Obama again.'

'Yeah, of course! Everyone in America is getting totally inspired. Why can't we have a bit of Obama magic over here?'

She frowned but I could see that she was warming to the idea. 'So what have you done so far?'

'There's this meeting happening next week – the one I told you about. I'm hoping there'll be about twenty people coming.'

'And what about before then?'

'Uhmm...'

'You're going to need permission aren't you, to have a rally in Parliament Square?'

'I guess so.'

'Have you got any money for banners and signs?'

'Not really.'

'What about insurance?'

'Nope. Do we need it?'

'Tamsin! Do you know anything about putting on events?'

'No,' I said, feeling a bit stupid and wondering how she knew so much about it all. 'Hey, wasn't your job project management? Oh, c'mon Lotti, manage this project, this is exactly what you quit work to do!'

She pursed her lips and tilted her head side-to-side like she was weighing the offer up. I hoped she was teasing me. 'Oh alright then.' She broke into a smile.

'Yeah!' I gave her a big hug – her willingness to get involved felt like such a gift. 'Let's make this amazing!'

Her hair had all fallen down and she began playing with it again. 'So, really basically, what needs to happen before October 13th?'

'We need to get people to come and we need to make sure that there's an event to come to.'

'So networking and project management. Okay, that's straight-forward. I'll be the project manager and you can be the event co-ordinator.'

I liked my title a lot. Everything felt much more real with two of us. She had her laptop with her so, armed with our new job descriptions, we turned on our computers, connected to the wireless network and logged into Facebook. After a guilty five minutes checking our messages we snapped to attention. Lotti started looking up the rules about protests in Parliament Square. I started thinking about the actual event – it had to be more than just a big crowd with someone shouting 'Rush!' at 6:30pm. We needed a build up, something to get the crowd buzzing. We were going to need high-profile speakers to address the crowd, a stage and sound system and, most importantly, police permission.

Lotti took on this aspect of the event. She was called into Scotland Yard, where she accepted legal responsibility for the whole thing, and she organised a fundraiser to raise the cash needed for 'public liability insurance'. Both of us worked at it for free, and both of us worked harder than we'd ever worked before.

The next week I was preparing for our first open meeting when my phone rang. It was Sam, the girl who'd said she'd help us out with getting a room that night:

'Hey Tamsin, I've had my ear to the ground and it doesn't look as though people are all that keen on this woman's action group.'

I'd been pretty jubilant. I'd been thinking from that evening onwards Lotti and I were going to be getting some help. The idea that no-one was going to turn up to this open meeting pulled the air from my gut. I opened my brother's front door with my free hand and stepped out onto the street. Sam continued:

'And I haven't been able to book a room.'

'What?!'

'So I guess you'd better cancel it.'

'No.' I said stubbornly, though I felt like the wind had been completely taken out of my sails. 'No, I'll work something out.'

I hung up the phone, and started rolling a cigarette. My brother came out to join me, 'What's wrong?'

I told him what Sam had said.

'I guess I've got to cancel it.'

'But how can you?'

'Dunno.' I kicked the step in annoyance. 'Ohhh, it's not going as I planned it!'

'Tamsin, get a grip! Why does her opinion even matter? Just because she's being negative doesn't mean she's right. If anyone's going to get some stupid hare-brained plan together in six weeks it's you. I thought disorganised spontaneity was what you did best.'

'But what if no-one turns up tonight?'

'Look, all the people you hang out with are really busy, so maybe they won't want to give their time to this – but just go tonight and check if anyone wants to get involved. If you don't believe it'll happen then nobody else will. Stop worrying and just get on with it!'

I spend a lot of time in my own head and I need people around me who have the common sense to pull me out of it. I went back inside, switched on my computer and began data-basing mother and toddler groups again.

Lotti and I arrived at the meeting with a list of things we needed: a media team, a legal team, a project management team and a networking team. I'd organised club nights with some of the girls coming along and I knew they'd be great at getting the event moving.

Lotti and I put a sign on the office Sam had failed to book a room in, saying that we were in the pub down the road. We found the biggest table and took up two of eleven places, telling disgruntled customers they couldn't take the chairs because we were expecting more people, we hoped. By 7:15pm every seat had been filled. The meeting began.

Liz, a scenester from East London, sat down next to me and started pouring out wine into the glasses in front of her. 'Have you thought about the look of the event?'

I took the glass she offered. 'We're definitely encouraging people to come dressed as Suffragettes.'

'So what – big hats, skirts, a lot of lace? That'll look great and it'll totally blind-side the police. They can't whack out the batons for a load of fabulously dressed women.'

'What about men?' This was Rachel, a girl I'd met at Climate Camp. 'This isn't a women-only thing, right?'

'No no, not at all,' I said. 'I guess it's Edwardian themed.'

'Wait a second,' said Marie, who'd volunteered to be our legal advisor. 'Does everyone have their phones off?'

'It's on silent,' said Emily, a friend of my brother's.

'No, it needs to be off, with the battery out.'

'Oh...' she said, taking out her phone and switching it off. Her sister Alice, sat to her right, did the same. 'Why's that?'

'It's just a security thing,' I said. 'Sometimes the police can listen in to conversations.'

The sisters looked at each other, like they weren't quite sure what they'd got themselves in to. I understood why we had to take precautions like that, but it did seem a bit ridiculous, especially as our conversation turned to accessories. 'Have you thought about having a sash?' said Liz.

'It's a bit Miss World isn't it?' This was Jenny, a friend Lotti had brought along.

'Yeah, exactly. We can reclaim it! It's about time it became a feminist statement again.'

I smiled at Liz, remembering all the pictures of Suffragettes I'd seen with their slogan 'Votes For Women'. She continued:

'What's our colour scheme?'

I took a sip of my drink. 'Didn't the Suffragettes use purple, green and white?'

The conversation started to flow more freely.

'Green – we should definitely still use green.'

'But we shouldn't just use the same colours...'

'White is really classic and really easy to find.'

'Green and white then.'

'Purple, though? I look terrible in purple.'

'What about red? Red for emergency.'

'Red for danger. We're coming and we're dangerous!'

I beamed at Rachel. I definitely liked the idea of being dangerous. Liz went on:

'So, what if we have people in white wearing red sashes?'

There was a general noise of agreement.

'What about screen printing them with our demands?' Emily suggested. 'Just like the Suffragettes.'

Nicole, a mum about twenty years older than the rest of us, swigged her wine. 'What exactly are our demands?'

A fresh conversation. My friend Jen, who'd been with me at the first Climate Camp, took over. She was working as a policy writer and quickly brought us up to speed on the major environmental issues facing government. She had an impressive back catalogue of facts, and soon we had a list of possible demands:

- 'NO THIRD RUNWAY' (at Heathrow Airport)
- 'NO NEW COAL' (no new coal-fired power stations)
- 'REFORM CLIMATE POLICY' (80% cuts by 2050 and investment in green technologies and infrastructure)

'We should have a more generic slogan as well,' said Nicole. 'One that says something like "EMERGENCY" or "Climate change is coming really fast and is going to completely mess up your entire life!".'

'I'm not sure that'll fit on a sash...' Emily said with a wry smile. A short conversation later and we'd come up with a fourth and final message for our sashes: 'CLIMATE CODE RED'.

Back to the appearance of the event: Emily and her sister Alice held court over this section of the meeting. They carefully articulated their ideas, and soon it was clear that if we wanted a new mass movement then they wanted to be in charge of its design.

'We'd really like to redo the flier,' said Alice, with a look I couldn't read.

'Oh, right,' I said. 'Well I'll send you over the original file of the one I did, if you want to start with that.'

The sisters looked at each other, and I could see them trying not to smile. 'I think we'd rather start from scratch.'

The whole table started laughing. I guess my flier was pretty lame.

The design conversation continued – there was so much that I hadn't even thought about. Alice seemed shy but her eyes were fiercely alive as she began to put her name next to tasks. She and Emily backed each other up and took on a lot: screen-printing over five hundred sashes, designing a logo and a silhouette look for the website, trawling round charity shops in search of Suffragette-style hats and dresses.

What about the media strategy? Rachel and Nicole both had a background and contacts in the PR world and seemed really excited at this idea of re-branding the green movement. Their eyes had a glint I recognized, that said, 'I understand this system and by God am I gonna work it!' – you don't often see that look on the faces of environmental activists, but it would be an essential tool if we were ever going to capture the attention of the rest of society.

Speakers? We brainstormed and came up with an ambitious wish-list: Green MEP Caroline Lucas; Samantha Roddick, daughter of Anita – the founder of The Body Shop – and a full-time activist in her own right; Fay Mansell, Head of the Woman's Institute, that most British of institutions; Rosie Boycott, feminist extraordinaire. Annie Lennox? Germaine Greer? Joanna Lumley? The list went on and on.

Three bottles of wine were shared round as we came up with networking ideas, media stunts, and talked through legal issues. There was so much to get done, but between eleven slightly tipsy women it suddenly felt so easy and so possible. We were a mixed group, and none of us were exactly experts, but we were buzzing off each other's presence and belief, and the feeling that we all had something to offer. We closed the meeting, ordered another bottle of wine and toasted the beginning of the Climate Suffragettes.

I spent most of the month between that meeting and the day of the Rush data-basing women's groups and sending out an endless stream of invite emails. From time to time I'd be invited to speak to a group of feminists or students, a church or a school. I'd use these opportunities to talk about this new vision of climate activism, when women would take charge and make it properly mainstream. Then I'd give them fliers and stickers. They could support our Rush by turning up on the night, but they could also network it themselves, put stickers up along their local high street and get a team together to make a banner.

I'd heard from my friends in Plane Stupid about some women

from West London who had launched an action group: weCAN. They'd held a vigil in Parliament Square some months before in protest against the third runway, and my friends thought they might be interested in the Climate Rush. Their leader, Nicole, had been at the first Rush meeting and she'd begun working on the media PR for the event. One day she called me to invite me to come to a weCAN meeting.

I arrived by bike at a classy coffee shop near Notting Hill and looked around the gathered group. I immediately felt intimidated. They were all twenty years older or so, definitely wiser and much more stylish. They were part of the generation of women who'd pushed through the glass ceiling into the highest paid, VIP jobs. They were even more impressive than the slick city girls I remembered from the milk round. Rosie Boycott, one of the women we hoped would speak at the Climate Rush, was sitting at the end of the table. I felt a little star-struck. What could I possibly have to say to such an empowered bunch?

As I talked them through the idea of the Rush the women glanced at each other round the table with smiles. It seemed as though this event was precisely the sort of thing that they'd launched their group to do. Rosie agreed to speak at the Rush without a second thought, and all of the women said they would network it. They were all freaked about their kids' futures. The conversation that we had in that coffee shop convinced me, more than anything else, that change is possible. Unlike the others who were on board planning the Rush, these were the kind of women you'd expect to deny climate change. They all enjoyed the lifestyles that our society makes possible. They had a high standard of living, and yet they were there, squaring up to the reality that the lifestyle they'd spent years securing just wasn't sustainable anymore. These people were tax-paying, law-abiding citizens. They probably never imagined they'd want to organise events that would push the boundaries of the law, but their fears for their children had prompted them to make their voices heard.

It felt like such an honour to be talking to such powerful women, people who were prepared to change their lives if it meant they could make a difference to climate change. They were well-connected, and before I left them I was given the direct number of Caroline Lucas MEP. She's the leader of the Green Party and one of the women that we really wanted to come and speak at the pre-Rush rally.

I left a lot of messages on her machine and I followed them up with emails for good measure. After a couple of days (time was so short) I gave up and began to focus on the other speakers. Rosie Boycott had confirmed but we desperately needed a representative of the Women's Institute and some sort of celebrity activist, the female version of George Monbiot. While rattling an email off to Sam Roddick my phone rang from a 'private number'.

'Hi, is that Tamsin Omond?'

'Speaking.'

'This is Cath, PA to Caroline Lucas. I'm just calling to let you know that Caroline will be able to join you on the 13th and is free to speak if you'd still like her to.'

'Yes, of course! Thank you so much.'

'Not a problem. Call me if you need anything else,' and she hung up the phone.

Immediately, I had a million questions. Most importantly, would Caroline close the rally and did she understand that in closing the rally she would be launching the rush? We definitely needed her speech to uplift the crowd and push them towards Parliament. I called Lotti immediately to share the news. I was elated. I'd seen Caroline speak at a climate demo the year before and I knew she had the power to inspire a crowd. Less than a year ago I'd watched 10,000 people drenched by rain and severely disheartened brought alive by her words. She had spoken clearly about the climate crisis, spelling out what it would mean for each of us in the not too distant future. Then I had heard her articulate why this was also an amazing opportunity for change. Since then she has transformed the Green Party. She's the first female leader of a party since Margaret Thatcher, and the first ever leader of the Greens. Society is finally beginning to take notice of their party, and Caroline recognized that they needed a leader to hone their direction and give them focus. Since then she has been relentlessly campaigning in Brussels and Westminster for environmental considerations to be at the heart of national and international policy. She's a mighty woman and it was so exciting that she'd decided that the Climate Rush was worth being involved with.

That evening I 'googled' Caroline Lucas and discovered that she also held a doctorate. She'd 'done' academia and was now making her mark in the political sphere. As I read on, getting ever more impressed, a realization dawned. Throughout the time I'd spent as a parish administrator I'd been studying for an MA in 'Environment and Social Policy'. While I'd been networking the Climate Rush I had basically forgotten about it. Academia had been put on hold because I thought what I was doing was more important – which was all well and good, but in side-lining my MA I'd totally forgotten my final exam was coming up really soon. I stopped 'googling' Caroline and signed on to the Open University homepage. I scrolled down to check when the exam would be and then I choked with laughter. October 13th. Right. On the day when I should have been taking sashes and banners down to Parliament Square I was also supposed to be sat in a university hall in Mile End sitting my final MA exam. Perfect.

I promised myself that tomorrow I would begin studying again. Then I remembered that I was supposed to be spending the whole next day out in London doing stunts to publicise the Rush. We'd already used the original Suffragette tactic of wandering around London with a piece of chalk each, dressed up as 21st century Suffragettes. Whenever we found an empty bit of wall or prominently placed pavement we would duck down and write out the details of our Climate Rush. Earlier in the week we'd done it outside a nightclub in Soho. A guy came out of his shop and asked what we were up to in our Edwardian garb. Alice explained and he seemed really touched that we were bothering to do something. I heard her ask, all coy, whether he would come along. He was so sweet and excited. Emily noticed that the shop he'd come out of was a hairdresser's and whispered something in her sister's ear. They giggled and smiled at him. He was still enthusing about how fabulous it was that we were dressing up as Suffragettes and hadn't seemed to notice the girls' ploy.

'I love your hairstyle,' Alice said.

'Oh, thanks!' the hairdresser smiled.

'Do you get your hair cut in your shop?'

'Yes, of course. My friend Marco cut it last week.'

She gave him a big smile. 'But I bet you're a better hairdresser than him, right?'

He laughed. Alice ran her hands through her hair and shrugged, then looked back sweetly at his shop. 'I wish I had better hair. Sometimes I really feel that we're letting the original Suffragettes down. They were so, so stylish and...'

She didn't continue, instead dejectedly tugged at her hair.

Then the penny dropped. The hairdresser smiled, shrugged and then became very animated and invited Alice into his shop. She smiled nodded and squeezed her sister's hand. We were all gob-smacked by her audacity. We continued to give out fliers as we chalked our message on Soho's walls and waited for Alice. A couple of times we went to watch through the window at a posse of hairdressers fussing over her and laughing at whatever she was saying. Eventually she was ready. We'd gone round the corner to hand out more fliers when she walked over to us. She had beautiful, sleek, dyed black hair.

That evening had been such a success. We'd felt like we'd really made our presence felt on the streets of Soho, and that lots of the people we'd spoken to would be there on the 13th. Someone had come up with the idea of trying something closer to the Houses of Parliament. I finished my email to Sam Roddick, wrote a press release, made a few more calls and then went to bed – it was going to be an early start the next day.

When I arrived at St James Park station the following day I was a little worried that no-one else would bother turning up. We were meeting the *Evening Standard* photographer at 9am sharp next to Winston Churchill and we needed to change and prepare. It was already 8:49am. Then I saw Emily, and Alice with her, and soon there was a group of seven of us hurrying to an alley-way where we quickly hauled our white frills on. I caught my reflection in a window and felt pretty silly. But the crowd was moving and as I looked around me I felt so incredibly proud of the group I was with: strikingly-dressed and on a mission.

As we approached Winston I saw the photographer and waved. He followed us as we sized up the statue. Emily put her knee against the plinth's base and told me to climb up. I put one foot down on her leg and pushed myself up against the statue. More hands met beneath my feet and pushed me up on the edge of the plinth. As I hauled myself up, the loose frilly skirt got caught and started getting pulled down over my bum. Fortunately Natalia, one of the weCAN mothers, saved my modesty by grabbing the elastic waistband from behind my back and yanking it back up over my hips. I pulled myself onto the plinth and crouched between Winston's legs.

Alice passed up the extra-long sash she'd made, and I now tried to get the five-metre-long sash around the hulking mass of Winston's body. I had a long stick to help me hook the sash around his neck but it soon became clear that we'd underestimated quite what a big man Winston was. There was no way that I was going to be able to reach around his shoulders, so instead I waved the sash in front of his nose a little before settling for tying it loosely around his foot.

Job done. The *Evening Standard* photographer was happy, and our team of Climate Suffragettes was super excited. We hurried to Nelson Mandela, on the other side of the square, and easily draped a sash around his shoulders and placed one in his open arms. It was fun walking away from that square feeling like we had already made our mark on Parliament. In less than two weeks we would be back, this time en masse.

***

Two weeks later, a miracle: the only three questions I could have answered all were all there on my MA exam paper. I whizzed through them as fast as I could, keeping a close eye on the time, and at 4.30pm exactly I put down my pen and half ran out of the room. Everyone else was still head-down at their desks, scribbling away. The invigilators looked a little surprised that I was leaving with an hour of the exam still left to go, but nobody stopped me. Outside, Mile End was busy. I unlocked my bike and worked my way into the traffic. It was half an hour's ride to Parliament and all the way my soul was singing.

CLIMATE RUSH

On Monday 13th October a number of environmental groups are associating themselves with the 100th anniversary of the 'Rush on Parliament' by the Women's Suffrage Movement in an event entitled 'Climate Rush'. This will involve a demonstration on Parliament Square during the afternoon and a planned 'Rush on Parliament' at 6:30pm.

A number of security measures will be implemented in order to maintain access for Members of both Houses and to mitigate disruption to Parliamentary business. Some of these – such as increased police presence within and around the Parliamentary Estate, a heightened search regime and the closure of the Victoria Embankment and Derby Gate Library entrances all day on 13th October – may inconvenience Members and staff. We would be grateful for your understanding.

Jill Pay
Sergeant at Arms

Sir Michael Willcocks
Black Rod

The Climate Rush was to begin at 6pm. I arrived early to set up the stage and PA. It was all hands on deck, rushing around Parliament Square and hoping that more people would arrive. At quarter to six people began to flood into the square. They were getting off buses at the top of Victoria Street and coming out of the various Westminster Tube exits. Some were dressed as Suffragettes, others wore their normal clothes, a handful were carrying banners and everyone was wearing a sash. My mum came up behind me. She whispered in my ear, 'It's about to start...' As I looked around I felt very proud, and my mum squeezed my hand. The speeches were just beginning and I was on a high.

Rosie Boycott began: 'A hundred years ago, to the day, our grandmothers did extraordinary things – quite how extraordinary they were not able to appreciate. We protest today, we invoke their spirit, because there must be dramatic action on climate change. She was followed by the deputy-chair of The Women's Institute. They'd recently published a report defining climate change as a women's issue. She told the crowd about the women the world over who were already suffering from climate change, before asking the women there to think about climate change in their every day lives.

Ismet Rawat spoke as a solicitor and member of the Association of Muslim Lawyers. She had come to tell us about the way that the law can change, that it should express our ideals and hopes for society. She had planned to speak about the way direct action challenged out-of-date laws and could highlight areas where new legislation was needed. But standing before the crowd, she didn't read her prepared speech. She was so touched by the number of women who had brought their families along that she spoke to the crowd as a mother, terrified for her children's future, hoping and praying that the laws which protected the corporate carbon emitters would change in time to avert catastrophe.

Big Ben, looming behind the stage, chimed 6:30pm It was almost time for the Rush. Caroline Lucas MEP was our final speaker and she ended her speech with a call to arms:

'Emmeline Pankhurst once said that to be militant is a privilege and by God she was right. Sisters, the time for words is over, the time for action is now.'

My mum beamed at me. It was time for her to go. 'And whatever you do, please DON'T get arrested...' She winked as she walked away.

***

Now I was walking towards the front of the crowd, passing green flags into its midst and manically waving my own. During one of the planning meetings we'd decided that green flag-waving would get the crowd going. Now I didn't feel so sure. There was a buzz but no-one was moving. We needed to be closer to Parliament, to be shouting our message to the people inside, to tell them that something was starting out here. But the police remained in place, boxing us in to Parliament Square and they were reinforced by the metal fencing that stood between us and them.

I overheard an elderly couple:

'Well? What happens now?'

He shrugged and they looked as though they might turn to go. I wanted them to know what could happen next.

I passed them my flag. 'Hey, why don't you carry this flag and get people moving that way?' I pointed them towards Parliament.

They smiled at me, probably bemused at my sudden involvement in their evening. I wanted to stay and tell them how I'd been involved in it all from the start, but there was no time – more people needed to be waving flags, more noise needed to be made, or we would never have the momentum to break through the police barricades and onto the road. I laughed as I watched the old man vigorously waving his flag and telling much younger people around him that they should be rushing towards Parliament.

To the left of Parliament Square a group of women, all wide-brimmed hats and wrapped in white, were smiling sweetly at the police as they lifted the barricades and walked out onto the road. It had begun. I saw Emily and Alice nearby and we grabbed the metal and lifted it out of the way.

About ten metres to the left another group was grappling with the fencing and pushing past police. My heart did something pretty special. I hadn't expected to see the weCAN mums on the frontline. Now they were blocking traffic and ignoring the police. Nicole caught my eye and smiled, and I knew that if these women were willing to take such daring steps then we weren't being ridiculously naïve to believe that the world could change.

The police seemed to be at an utter loss. Women, men and children were breaking out from the boundaries of Parliament Square. Soon there were a thousand people in the road, heading for Parliament's huge oak doors. From behind me a shout went up. It was the old Suffragette slogan: 'DEEDS NOT WORDS!'. The two sisters grabbed me and together we were leading the crowd. I looked to my left and saw two faces beaming back. We yelled, 'DEEDS NOT WORDS!' and heard it yelled back from the crowd behind. We were eye-to-eye with a line of police but there was nothing they could do to stop the surge. I stopped trying to look back and instead fixed my eyes on the police officer in front of me and the door to Parliament which lay beyond.

The heavy oak doors of St Stephen's Gate were slammed shut and

I could hear the thump as heavy bolts were dropped. What were they doing? If they closed that entrance then there would be a thousand-strong crush against their door. For the first time that night I was scared, worrying that the weight of all these people would mean someone getting hurt. The police were powerless against us but if they penned us into a tiny area then who knew what would happen in the crush. The police threw some metal fencing against the crowd and it crashed down on a friend's leg. They then charged towards the crowd without noticing that they were stomping on the spot where her leg was still trapped. An ambulance was called and she was dragged from the crush. This was the absolute worst case scenario – three bones were broken and she would be off work for nine months. As the ambulance flashed away I wondered how Steph would feel about the action having such an impact on her life.

A samba band struck up and there was now a rhythm to the shouts of 'DEEDS NOT WORDS!'. We were yet to reach the doors but soon, very soon, the police would have to step back. To my right a boy, dressed in a white skirt, frilly shirt and light blue hat, had broken through the police line and was knocking hard against the door:

'Let us in. Let us in. Deeds not words. Deeds not words. DEEDS NOT WORDS!'

I wanted to thump my fists on it too. I reached beyond the police line and touched the door.

'Right Tamsin, you're nicked.' An officer was lifting me high above the protesters and the police line. He shoved me against the wall and forced cuffs around my wrists. My face was pushed into the wooden frame of the door and – even though I'd known this would happen if I went in this close to Parliament – I somehow couldn't believe I was being arrested. He then spun me round so that I was on the top step before St Stephen's door. Directly in front of me were around forty police in fluorescent yellow jackets, and behind them one thousand climate activists, more or less uniform in white crossed with a bright red sash.

I had never allowed myself to imagine what the Rush might actually be like. I hadn't dared to believe that the people who turned up, some known to me, most of them strangers, would get so excited that at the final hurdle they would fulfil our greatest expectations and actually rush at Parliament. No amount of forward planning could have ensured this moment. Either people were going to feel it, take a risk and rush, or they would retreat, listen to the speeches, sign the petition and leave. I'd hoped so much that we would give the Suffragettes an anniversary worthy of their own actions, but I'd never really believed that we could. From my step above the crowd I could see the police's yellow line, and beyond them were people, a lot of people, all facing Parliament. There was a crush along the pavement and further back the road around Parliament Square, all three lanes, was blocked by the crowd.

The roar went up:

'DEEDS NOT WORDS!'

and I was led away.

***

'How dare you drag this woman along the ground!'

'Sorry sir,' said the Inspector as he pulled me to my feet and brushed me down just outside another door to Parliament.

This man, grey-haired and with sharp blue eyes, put out his hand to shake mine. He saw my arms trapped behind my back and let his outstretched hand fall to the ground. He shrugged and smiled: 'I'm John McDonnell, MP for Sipson, the village that this government will demolish to make way for Heathrow Airport. It's a pleasure.'

I smiled back at him. 'Tamsin Omond.'

'They're all talking about it in there you know. We're not allowed to leave the chamber! It's been an hour now and who knows how long they'll last,' he gestured to the roars of the Rush. 'You're making climate change more and more difficult to ignore. Well done.'

I beamed back at him, too shy to speak.

***

At the police station Molly, a PC who I've met at countless demos since, booked me in. In another life she could have been a Suffragette. She is strong and inspired by what she does. She is the compassionate face of the police force and I like to think of her as a friend. Even if she arrests me again in the future I think that each of us respects what the other does. There are so many laws that should be fiercely upheld. I only hope that one day the laws she fights to protect will include legislation against the worst of the carbon emitters. When she booked me in I asked her about the consequences of breaking bail. I'd broken the conditions I'd been given after the Plane Stupid banner drop and I'd heard that it would definitely mean a trip to Holloway – where I'd have to wait two months until my trial for trespassing on the roofs of Parliament.

She reassured me. The judge would be lenient – after all, I was only protesting. I hoped that what she said was true. Two months alone in prison seemed unimaginable. Taking action as part of a group where we were all prepared to face the same consequence makes you part of a community. Being arrested by yourself means you lose that support. Of course, there are people outside the prison's walls who are thinking of you, praying for you and generally wishing you well. But it is not the same as knowing that the cells around you are filled with your friends.

For that night though, alone in the cell, I was jumping from the walls. The energy and success of the Rush had kicked off my adrenaline and I wondered how I would quieten down so I could get some sleep. I felt ecstatic, but also jealous. It seemed unfair that everyone else was still outside Parliament partying away, or out in the pub toasting their entry into history. I toasted them too, with my Styrofoam cup of sugary tea.

The following morning I was taken from the police station to court. It was strange not to be one of a group of fellow activists. I shared the ride with the other inmates of Paddington Green. We looked at one another with a degree of mistrust. I suppose they must have been stifling laughter at this girl dressed in a long white pleated skirt, a frilly shirt and a red sash. When we arrived we were divided up and I was taken to my cell. I was put in a cell with a woman on day release from Holloway. I gulped, smiled and took up my corner in the room.

I was eyed up and down and scowled at. There was silence.

'I can't be left alone in a cell. I have fits.'

Perfect.

'Not crazy fits. Just can't be in a cell by myself. Once they put me in solitary. Had to let me out after a day. I was cut and bruised all over.'

Gulp, smile, silence.

'You're a quiet one aren't you?'

Smile. Silence.

'What you in for?'

'I broke my bail conditions last night.'

'Shit, so you'll be heading to Holloway this evening? They're gonna love you there.' Again, she eyed me slowly up and down.

'Do you think that's true? I thought… Well, I thought that it might depend…'

'No, the judge'll be fucked off. They get grumpy when you break bail. It'll be a week and then you can appeal and then maybe your lawyer'll pull something off, maybe.'

There's so much that stands in the way of doing good things. Uncomfortable hours in a cell with a woman whose life has been so very different from your own. Two months in prison, away from your friends. Or just the end of your hopefulness, your faith that you can change anything.

It was sad sitting in a cell with this woman who had spent the past seven years in Holloway and had at least eleven more to go. Her eyebrows lifted when I explained that I was inside for eco-protests, that I would risk jail for something so distant, something that seemed so unreal to her. I knew that I was sounding like an idiot, a posh little twit with lofty ideas. It seemed ridiculous to talk about climate change as she fished through her pants, pulling out a rollie wrapped in cellophane, three pills and a match. She lit the match against the wall (she was a pro), sucked on the rollie and downed the pills.

'If you sign onto the rehab ward they give you three jabs a day and pills on top of that! It's really not so hard. Don't worry about it. twenty-four hour cable TV and a regular supply. There's a reason why people reoffend.'

She winked and fell asleep.

I don't remember what I thought about from my corner of the cell. I was scared, but I didn't really believe I'd be sent down. I remember wondering how I'd ever get away with wearing a Suffragette outfit if I was packed off to Holloway. I thought a bit about spending two months high on whatever cocktails of drugs they would give me to pass the time. I wondered what hope there was and whether people can change.

When I was finally called to court the judge played with me a little. I stood in the dock, and glanced at my friends who had come to give me support. I tried to look brave and resolute, like a real Suffragette would have done. The judge's stern gaze brought me back to the real world. Actions do have consequences and it finally hit me that prison was a very real possibility. As my cellmate had said, I'd pissed him off and he had the power to make me pay. On any other day her prediction might have become a reality. But sometimes, just sometimes, stories can inspire something different. District Judge Michael Snow ruled that I had broken my bail conditions and that I was in 'grave peril' of being taken into custody. I held my breath and waited for his final words. 'I recognise a need for proportionality and one should hesitate from taking away bail from someone exercising their right to protest.'

I left the court and joined my friends outside.

⌛ TIME BOMB: *Peak Oil*

It looks as though climate change isn't the only apocalyptic problem on the horizon... 'Peak oil' is one of those phrases you hear around but nobody seems to know what it means. People in the movement don't really talk about it that much – maybe they think it will confuse people, or maybe they don't want to draw attention to an issue which has so much uncertainty around it.

Some people use 'peak oil' to mean the moment where more than half of all the oil in the world has been extracted. Some say it's when the amount we're using is more than we can get out of the ground. Nobody really knows how much oil exists because most of it is owned by national governments who are very secretive about their reserves.

But we can be sure of three things:

- Oil is finite. It will run out one day.
- We are using more and more of it and we use it for pretty much everything. We are totally dependent on it.
- Like climate change, there's a lot of deliberate misinformation as well as proper scientific debate. And like climate change, that debate has pretty much been settled in the last couple of years, with most companies, organisations and individuals saying the same sort of thing.

Whatever your particular definition of 'peak oil', our ever-increasing thirst for it can't continue forever. This means that some day we have to find a way of living with much less of it, or without any at all.

When is it going to happen?

- In 2006 the International Energy Agency said that people talking about peak oil were 'scare-mongerers'. Its 2008 report said that world production of conventional oil would peak or plateau in 2020.
- CEOs of BP and Conoco have given the date of the peak between 2010 and 2020.
- Dr Colin Campbell, the former chief geologist and vice-president of BP, Shell, Fina, Exxon and ChevronTexaco says that the peak of cheap oil happened in 2005, while the peak of harder to extract forms of oil will come in 2011.
- The Peak Oil Group, a set of British companies including Virgin, Yahoo and Scottish and Southern Energy, commissioned a report on peak oil. They concluded the peak would arrive in 2013.

Planning for a world with less oil is going to take years. Even if we've got until 2020 it's still really, really soon.

What will the effects be?

Oil is used in everything. Literally everything. The water that comes out of your taps has been purified in a refinery powered by oil. The taps were made in a factory powered by oil. The plastic fittings inside were made directly from oil and transported by truck across the country to the shop using petrol made from oil, which you travelled to in a car or a bus powered by oil. Even the manufactures of your bicycle used oil when it was made.

In Britain most of our farmland is so poor that pretty much nothing grows without the aid of fertilizers made from oil.

Some things can be replaced with other fossil fuels, but at the moment our transport all runs on liquid fuels made from oil. We do have the technology to replace it with electric transport but this will take time.

If the supply chains shut down we have enough food in Britain to feed ourselves for about three days.

Some people think that the issue of climate change is so much bigger than peak oil that peak oil doesn't really matter. Others think that peak oil is coming so much sooner than climate change that it should be our first concern. The problem is, if you only think about one you'll make the other loads worse. If all our solutions to climate change involve huge global projects like geo-engineering and carbon capture and storage, how are we going to power them when the oil runs out? And if we only have big solutions to peak oil, like making coal and gas into liquid fuels, how can we have any hope of reducing our carbon emissions? Actually, the solution to one is the solution to both.

We have to have local communities that can produce lots of

their own food and energy, don't rely on long supply chains and are still connected to other communities but not so dependent on them.

My housemate is involved in Hackney Transition Town. She organises seedling swaps and environmental film screenings and she's even helped set up a LETS scheme where local people trade their time instead of money. This is a different sort of action to activism – not many people in Transition Towns want to get arrested, and most of them still live in the real world, among people who aren't that green and don't want to change their lives. That bridge is so important and I admire them for doing something.

But there are some things local communities can't do on their own. They can't change national policy. They can't stop the rainforests being cut down. They can't make sure that the world's climate migrants find a place to go when their homes are flooded. Yes, we need grass-roots communities teaching people to grow their own food, insulate their houses and care for their neighbours. If that's your cup of tea (flown all the way from India) then look up your local Transition Town because it is really important. But this is not enough on its own. We also need to be talking to the people in power, through direct action.

CHAPTER FIVE

LIGHT STREAMS THROUGH MY WINDOW AND I PULL
the crumpled blankets over my face. I'm not ready for morning – I
whack my alarm silent and shut out the brightness. Turned to the wall
I breathe deeply, clinging to the last minutes of a dream: thousands of
faces, each one different, but the same smile on every face.

There's an incredible optimism to my dream that seems to fit this
morning's world. I'm in bed, definitely dreaming, but the images
are reminding me of something, something my mind keeps glancing
over, almost catching, then losing hold of. The question itself starts
to properly wake me up: what is so special about today?

A thought clarifies, then a feeling, and suddenly I've got it, I've
remembered: Obama is inaugurated today. The promise of hope
and celebration shakes me awake and I leap out of my nest: sheets,
duvets, blankets – a cocoon of warmth in a house of students eager

to reduce heating bills.

Pulling on sweater-after-jumper-after-shirt-after-vest I step out of my room and into the 8am bustle of the waking house. I can hear music from downstairs and the sounds of my housemates thumping around the kitchen and singing along:

'Sometimes I feel like saying, "Lord I just don't care!" But you've got the love I need to see me through.'

I run downstairs and into the kitchen to join their dancing, leaping into the melee, a twisting whirl of seven girls and Apoc, joining, breaking, taking hands. It's the perfect shock to the system. My feet are incredibly cold, my heart incredibly warm, my brain snapped to alert.

This morning everything has changed. This morning the world is in love with one man's promise, a promise that speaks to us all. In my housemates' smiles I see my own ridiculous idealism reflected, the hope-against-hope that this might really be a politician we can believe in.

***

A guy in a hoodie is eyeing me up. It's not exactly threatening, but it is a little off-putting, especially on what I'd hoped would be the best day of my life. I'm running late. My toes are cold. I feel fed-up.

Rather than respond to his glances I try to stare out beyond the train tracks. But I can't help checking to see if he's still staring, which means we keep on catching each other's eyes, and now he winks at me. A cheeky smile flickers across his face and suddenly, against my better judgment, I'm laughing.

Which is, of course, a conversation starter:

'What d'you do?'

He's asked a good question. What do I do? I live in Clapton, rushing on my bike to meetings, cafés, actions. I don't work for an organisation and I don't have an employer, instead I'm sprinting every which way trying to create a buzz around the 'Climate Rush'. Does that make me an environmental campaigner? That'll just make him yawn. 'Green activist' – he'll take the piss. 'Eco-warrior'? But that even makes me laugh.

'Uhmm...' I make a noise about social change.

With feet-weight-shifting I look slightly away and when I look back he's taken out his phone. Crap. I've prompted one of those awkward situations: a crowded platform, a sense of stress and now the invasion of everyone's personal space. Anthony (who shakes my hand to introduce himself) stands as if unaware of conventional train platform niceties. Instead he has transformed his phone into a beat-box and begins spitting rap in my direction. The middle-aged lady behind him is watching guardedly and with definite disapproval. I feel responsible and want to apologise somehow.

But it's Anthony's laughing voice that draws me in: with lyrics and a tone that capture the ear. It's unexpected and seems out of place, but as it turns out, Anthony is really very good. Reading, spitting, singing, shouting poetry in all directions. The tinny beat of his phone keeps his rhythm and clarifies his rhyme. It's cool and I notice people beginning to nod along with him. The middle-aged woman's expression has shifted and younger people all along the platform are looking round.

The train pulls in and, smiling, we step in.

'What d'you wanna see change?'

'Uhmm…' (I hesitate for far longer this time, sometimes I hate talking to people about climate change.) 'Well, I want people to protect the environment.'

'No way! Check this, check this.'

(His enthusiasm is contagious. I'm grinning again, ready and waiting to check it:)

'Stuff more, don't stop, it's not time yet, there's one last mouthful,
let's fight for it, don't listen, shut up, slam the door,
break down for the fade-out of life's last call
and lies that we must win this war
whilst all stands broke and all just fall
out of broken dreams will come, another way, a different one
and where they lead we'll follow strong,
each broken rule a different song.
Love is new. We're back.'

I look around and notice that everyone is smiling. Middle-class mothers take one eye off their uniformed children to edge closer to this 'hoodie'. In their confused enjoyment the headlines about knife crime and gang warfare battle with their natural curiosity and interest. Anthony's spontaneous explosion of song has cut through the stereotype. He puts my daily efforts at persuasion to shame. He spits right up against despair and isolation but instead of alienating, boring or depressing us, he fills us with energy and hope. He has cut through the passive aggression of a crowded train, entered an indifferent space and filled it with his energy. I think of Obama and the global changes that are coming. Things will turn upside down and we will turn with them.

Anthony pauses and the stillness of the carriage is total. Everyone is intent on what this prophet has to say. A well turned-out woman breaks the silence.

'My husband owns a record label. I reckon he'd be really interested in you.'

Everyone's involved in this coincidence. All the people watching, listening to the song, have heard this woman's offer. The pair swap numbers: one twin-set, pearls and high-collared shirt; the other big cap, phone wire dangling from the ear and a bright yellow hoodie. It's difficult to imagine their worlds crossing except by accident.

The lady seems serious. She's asked him to introduce her to his manager. He looks bemused and then we work out that she means me.

'But I'm not his manager...' I understand her mistake. Why else would I, in my meeting clothes, black trousers, jacket and crisp white shirt, be hanging with this guy? We both smile and, talking one over the other, say that we just met, on the platform, waiting for the train – how can we explain that today the old borders have been erased? She smiles, embarrassed, and turns back to her find.

My mind leaps forward: one day I'll be descending the escalator, browsing adverts commanding me to buy this holiday, or that mascara, or some kind of 'confidence-boosting' plastic surgery. Then I'll catch sight of Anthony's latest release. I believe his passion will shine through the advertising gloss, that he'll still be completely himself even when he's being packaged and sold.

But how does he do it? I phase out further from his conversation with the woman in pearls. What can I learn? What was so special about the way he presented something that had been heard a thousand times before? He had made us remember that we're connected, that the walls and barriers we construct between us can change, can tumble, can open up new worlds.

This day is getting better. So many coincidences, surprises, moments of serendipity.

***

I'm less than ten minutes late for my appointment with the

ambassadors. Result! Finally, armed with assorted propaganda and fliers from the Climate Rush, I arrive at the studio where two hundred youngsters are eating a pizza lunch. Today is their award ceremony for having completed the 'young speakers' programme. This means that over the past year they have responded to social issues that touch their lives. Through the resources offered by 'wearewhatwedo.org' (Eugenie Harvey's brainchild) they have been directed by those with campaigning know-how and have launched their own youth movement. These two hundred kids, aged sixteen to eighteen, have spoken at hundreds of schools to over 40,000 of their peers. It's incredible to be in the midst of such an empowered crowd. A crowd which, when I arrive, is bouncing off the walls, racing around the room, screaming and laughing, hyped from caffeine, accomplishment and a morning spent sitting and listening. Their afternoon should be more fun, including a number of interactive workshops followed by the ceremony in the evening.

Eugenie appears beating a cattle-bell. Its hollow tone doesn't ring far above the racket. She resorts to the age-old teacher tactic and yells. Her strong, clear voice punches through the kids' chat. They shut up so quickly it's uncanny. This is clearly a woman they respect.

After a short introduction it is my turn to speak. The group is divided and I am going to run a workshop for thirty kids. I sit them in a circle and ask them to introduce themselves and suggest one action that they'd ask a million people to do.

Leanne: 'If I could ask one million people to do a simple action it would be to smile, it'd make the world a happier place.'

Theresa: 'I would ask one million people just to switch off anything that's not being used, like the TV, laptops, the light switches...and no more standby.'

Abigail: 'Get a double-sided printer to save paper, and don't use cars to get to work so there's less pollution.'

Nancy: 'Look around you! If we all open our eyes there's always something to be grateful for or smile about, even on a bad day. It can be something big like seeing someone you love or something small like seeing just one daisy in a patch of grass. It would make us all happier.'

Jessica: '...to tell at least one person one of the ways you can save electricity and also to smile and say something positive to someone at least twice every day.'

Nathan: 'Don't waste food – buy food for meals and not more 'cos you'll waste it.'

Zamilla: 'Tell someone how much they mean to you.'

Hirra: 'Stop using plastic bags. Or...turn off lights if you are not in the room.'

Mike: 'Put money in a fund to make the country greener and have more renewable energy.'

Nasreen: 'I would tell people to cut down on how many plastic bags they use, like reusing them or having other bags they can use again and again and again. This way WE CAN SAVE THE WORLD!'

Rachel: 'To give someone a hug until they get the fuzzy feeling… not in that way though!'

She bursts out laughing and so does everyone else.

The suggestions continue: all want to tell people either to do something to reduce their climate impact or do something to make the world a happier place. These teenagers understand that the two things are intertwined. They want to take responsibility for the world they live in and they want to transform it into a beautiful place. They know the defining issues of their generation and they know that the solutions involve us all. They want to make people change the way they act.

By the time my workshop is over the kids have decided to hold their own 'Rush' in the run up to the climate talks at Copenhagen in December. As well as changing their own habits, and encouraging their friends and families to change theirs, they will go to Parliament and demand that the government shows the leadership that is so desperately required: a leadership that would represent them and reflect their enthusiasm and imagination.

I leave the meeting with a new project and a new vision of what might be achieved. Parliament Square overrun with children, a youth occupation of our political space, empowered by their own vision and voice. The young calling for the old world to change.

***

This message has been written large in the media, filtered through Obama's PR campaign. Can we change? 'YES, WE CAN.' Are you sure? 'YES, WE CAN.' How will we do that? 'YES, WE CAN.' The slogan doesn't answer all of our questions but that's not what it's about. It creates a sense of excitement that finally something positive and empowering has come to the forefront of a distant political system.

The environmental movement has missed that trick. All too often we seem to be shouting the opposite. 'NO, YOU CAN'T – fly around the world, eat your favourite food, leave the lights on.' The optimism and enthusiasm of Eugenie's ambassadors is sometimes there but it can get lost in the messaging; most people seem to find environmentalists kind of depressing. It doesn't make caring about the environment seem very appealing. But it's hard to keep being positive when you understand what climate change really means.

People who know much more than me tell me, in the precise language of science, that my future will be lived in a world unrecognizable from the one we have now. These people have name-tags and white overalls and letters after their names. They have spent their lives researching climate change and their updates on the global situation seem ever more grim. But somehow it doesn't seem to penetrate. Even when people know the facts they don't wake up to what that means, which makes the situation all the more terrifying to face up to. The few who do wake up to reality freak out. Instead of getting mobilized and organised many people despair, because all they see is a world blindly heading for disaster.

There are days when I want to go back so much it hurts. Or else I want so much to close my eyes tight and disappear. No-one is dealing with what climate change really means. Politicians say they are, but when it really comes down to it, this is the lowest thing on the political agenda, even though it's the biggest threat to our future. Sometimes I have the energy to fight but sometimes everything's just black. I want to forget what I know about climate change. I want to be like the millions of other people who have things they find more important on their minds. I want to be able to ignore the possibility that these five years will be the last of their kind, and that after that we will be heading into a full-on collapse.

Sometimes it's so overwhelming you want to hide under your duvet, whack on some music at top volume and shut everything out. And sometimes it makes you reckless. I remember sitting in Hoxton Square one night with Phil, a really brilliant guy I'd met on a few 'actions' (which is what we call our protests). He was new to the movement like me, and although we didn't know each other that well he'd called me up after a bad day. His whole family had given up on their plans to get the train to Italy for a holiday and had booked flights to New York. It wasn't just that he couldn't go with them. He'd really thought that they were getting the message. They supported him when he was arrested and showed their faces at various actions. But by changing their holiday plans they proved just how far they were from really getting it.

I thought he needed cheering up, so we got a bottle of rum and drank it neat. Rum normally perks me up, but that day it just made us get more and more depressed. We kept trying to change the subject but everything led us back to climate change. The worst-case scenario suddenly seemed horribly real. Millions of people starving, millions more displaced, fortress Britain, a police state – it was so close we could almost touch it. Yet we were sitting there in the middle of London, with people walking past with bags of shopping from Tesco and Primark, and the lights were still on and the cars were still running, like nothing at all was wrong.

We got paranoid and took the batteries out of our phones – the police had had their hands on them and we thought someone might be using them to listen in – and now it was a different sort of conversation. What could we do about it? How far would we go? By the end of our rum-fuelled conversation we'd been to prison, gone on hunger strike, started a global movement, become Prime Minister, failed to start a global movement, claimed asylum in Canada and been martyred by the police. There was this kind of weird excitement in with the terror, like the feeling you get when you watch a horror film. We just kept looking at each other and saying 'Shit!' and taking another swig of rum and building up this horrific car-crash future that we couldn't look away from.

Eventually we decided to head home. We grabbed our bikes and started wobbling down Old Street through the Friday night traffic. At the cross roads I took a left, waving goodnight to Phil, and trying to focus on finding my way home. Then I heard shouts from behind me. Phil was having a noisy argument with the driver of a Hummer limousine – the vehicle was stopped in traffic and the driver was standing next to it and pointing at the side door. The window above it was open and three girls in pink tiaras were leaning out of it. I think the driver thought Phil had scratched the paint with his bike. Uh-oh. I knew nine-miles-to-the-gallon Hummers were a pet-hate of Phil's, and even if he wasn't the one who'd scratched it things might get ugly.

I pedalled back to see Phil leaning in towards the car and the driver shove him back. The girls inside shrieked with laughter. Phil half lost his balance, and as he righted himself I could see his whole body tense up, all the frustration of the evening wind itself into his fist. For an awful moment I thought he was going to smack the driver. Then he caught my eye as I sped up and instead he wheeled round and punched the wall behind him. Fist met brick with a sickening crunch. The girls gasped. I rushed up and hugged him as he nursed his hand. We spent six hours in A&E that night. He still has the scar on his knuckles.

I often think of that night when I start feeling overwhelmed. There's a fine line between the adrenaline-fuelled energy you get before an action and the desperation that leads to recklessness. And there's a fine line between desperation and despair. My father is Czech. He escaped the Communists in 1966, after being badly beaten, and once he told me a story about a different protest – the sort of protest that comes out of absolute futility, when the world is broken and there is no hope of it being fixed. In Czechoslovakia, at the beginning of the Russian occupation, a student called Palak walked to the centre of Prague. He stood in their most famous square: Wenceslas Square. He poured petrol over his body, clothes and hair. He lit and dropped a match.

As more people wake up to climate change, the sense that you are alone in your fears disappears and the truth of it becomes easier to bear. Communities of protesters get together and you can feel part of something positive. You make friends and talk about the terror and you laugh and imagine it won't be all that bad. But sometimes the craziness swamps you from all sides. You feel lost, you don't know where to turn, every action seems to make it worse, even the good ones turn out to be greenwashed – in this mess of intentions, the dousing of petrol and the lighting of one match could feel so pure, so simple and so honest. Sometimes I want to escape from this life and the future we've been promised.

Pretty weird, huh? And I've never even been suicidal. I'm actually an incredibly happy person. In every club there are girls with darker eye make-up than me and skinnier jeans. They glare when I beam. But we're not talking suicide. We're talking despair. The kind of despair that means every action you take is robbed of sense and purpose and hope. The kind of despair that makes action just symbolic. Climate change has transformed the future of our society but no-one has really changed: not in terms of their behaviour or their attitudes. From what we buy in the shops, to where we take our holidays, to whether we have children; everything has a carbon cost and a moral dimension, but it doesn't get talked about, at least not in any way that really acknowledges how far we have to change.

Soon there will be no point in hoping for a better future. Soon it will be too late to do anything to prevent climate change. All we will be able to do is react to increasingly impossible living conditions. But not yet: there is still hope in the months we have left before irreversible damage is done. There is still a point in fighting, even if the challenges can seem insurmountable. Young people all over the world are facing up to it and trying to change direction and there are still days when another world really does seem possible.

***

So back to Obama's inauguration day, with hope and sunshine in the air.

As I leave the ambassadors with a head filled with images of teenagers crowding into Parliament, I take stock of what's happened so far today: I have woken up to a joyful house, smiled in the sunlight, met a remarkable boy and a business matriarch, swapped plans with an empowered group of kids. I am totally content. Then there's a flurry of phone-calls: my friends have bought me a racing bike, an environmental foundation has donated £5000 to the Climate Rush and a club in Dalston wants to put on a 'Rush' night.

And now, the reason why I awoke with a buzz that would invigorate my day. It's 4:40pm: time to find Georgi and watch the inauguration.

Georgi and I are in love with Obama.

I'm first to arrive at the pub. It's empty apart from the usual suspects staring into their pints. As I walk into the bar their eyes lift questioningly. I ask that they turn on the big screen for Obama, and then I ask for a beer. The barman smirks a little, asks the regulars if they mind – there are shrugs all round, me thinking, 'Just you wait lads, this is going to be history...' – and the barman points the remote control at the TV to switch it on. I settle into my chair and watch.

Georgi enters as Obama is starting to speak. She sits on the arm of my chair with my hand in hers.

'Let it be told to the future world that in the depth of winter, when nothing but hope and virtue could survive, that the city and the country, alarmed at one common danger, came forth to meet it.'

He calls on the past, and he speaks for the future.

'America, in the face of our common dangers, in this winter of our hardship, let us remember these timeless words; with hope and virtue, let us brave once more the icy currents, and endure what storms may come; let it be said by our children's children that when we were tested we refused to let this journey end, that we did not turn back nor did we falter; and with eyes fixed on the horizon and God's grace upon us, we carried forth that great gift of freedom and delivered it safely to future generations.'

Obama closes and I glance round the room. The three Jamaican men who smirked as I walked in now sit tall, with smiles that light up the dingy pub. One has tears in his eyes and his drinking partners link themselves to him, one touching his wrist, the other his knee. It's tender, a sign of connection.

Georgi meets my gaze. I don't know what to say and neither does she. We look around the bar, smiling. Everybody is like us: silent, reflecting, full of hope.

Obama's words recall a spirit we had almost forgotten. He inspires memories of some other way of life. No one knows if all he promises is possible, yet it feels like Obama really does speak to a unified world. But what about the rest of us? How are we supposed to act in the face of all the opposition the world throws at us?

With compassion, I guess. Fellow-feeling and forgiveness.

There are simple examples in our world. From Anthony in a train carriage to the children I had met in school, all the way to the new President in the White House, people are walking to a different tune and transforming the world they see. Obama's influence may stretch further, but Anthony's wisdom, the children's determination and the choices made by the billions across the globe can also change the world.

These pages have more questions than answers. No-one can know where we are heading or how we will arrive. Instead, they aim only to express, in some small part, a universal faith so daunting that we almost fear its touch, the still small voice that fights in each of us.

CHAPTER SIX

The DIY Guide For The Climate Suffragette

THE SUFFRAGETTES BECAME POWERFUL BECAUSE THE medium was the message. Every time one of them got arrested she not only drew attention to their cause, she also contradicted her society's ideas about what women could be. In a world which told her she needed to depend on the protection of men she showed how empowered she already was. She wasn't asking them to give her the strength to survive prison or force-feeding during hunger strikes. She was asking them to recognise that she already had it.

In some ways the most impressive thing about the Suffragette movement was the fact that it managed to mobilise men, too. Two were arrested at the Suffragette Rush itself. These men had lived their whole lives with an advantage so total and so widespread that it was almost invisible. But once they had woken up to the injustice of this situation they wanted to share in the struggle, because they knew that both men and women suffered as a result of the inequality between them. They believed that marriages would be happier, children would be better brought up and everyone would be more prosperous if men and women could participate equally in society.

Those men were surrounded by women. They had mothers, wives, daughters, mistresses and maids. They had grown up being ruled by Queen Victoria. Yet it was still hard for them to see the hundreds of ways that half the population were disadvantaged by the law and by society. Today in the West, we're like those men. So many of the things we enjoy come at a cost to someone else. Right now there's the costs of poverty, disease, malnutrition – the result of some people taking more than their fair share, so there's less for the rest. And there's the costs of the not-so-distant future of climate change, when all the inequalities we see now will be made so much worse. In some ways it's easier for us to ignore global inequality, because the people we disadvantage the most live far away. They only touch our lives rarely, when we travel, or when they arrive at our borders looking for a better life. They don't live with us the way that Edwardian men lived with Edwardian women and it's easy for us to block them out. But in other ways it's just crazy to think that we can ignore it, because they outnumber us five-to-one.

I guess when I think about wanting to be like the Suffragettes I think of their bravery: how determined they were to make change happen; how successful they were; and how much poorer my own life would have been if they had failed. Around the world people are already mobilising over climate change but in the West we are hardly making a sound. A whole generation needs to show that they are already willing to make the changes needed to make the world a more just and beautiful place. We don't need empowerment, we need our power to be recognised! We can demonstrate this willingness through living out our ideals in places like Climate Camp or by making simple changes to our homes. And we can also show what sort of people we are through the sacrifices we are willing to make. The medium is the message.

Changing your consumer habits, your light bulbs and your mode of transport is important, but it won't change society. Yes, our lifestyles must publicise our concern about the environment, but so, too, must the shops that line our high street, the industries that fuel our economy and the banks that hold our cash.

A local group is your starting point. Gather a group together and then focus your attention outwards. There are industries and companies that will not change their carbon record without a lot of consumer pressure. Some industries never will. Petrol stations rely on petrol and supermarket chains rely on food imported by flights. If you organise campaigns that target high street companies and carbon-intensive industries you can raise awareness about what your local group is doing whilst publicising the climate impact of your target and the responsibility they must take. You might also disrupt the ease with which your target functions, sending a clear message both to the industry and the politicians: climate change is the greatest threat of all time and we will use every conceivable tactic to cut emissions.

It is extraordinary acts that inspire and transform society. These acts have to happen in your house and out in the street. We are all going to have to change, sooner or later, and the sooner we do it the easier it will be. If you disrupt someone's day job or their weekly shop then talk to them. Invite them to join the campaign and lend them a Climate Suffragette sash. Be courteous and target the corporation rather than the person whose wages they pay. We are not trying to remove jobs but create new ones that will build something for the future.

ACTION STATIONS

If you are going to take action as a community of Climate Suffragettes then the most essential campaigning item is the red climate sash. The original Suffragettes all wore a purple, white and green sash with their key slogan emblazoned across its front: 'VOTES FOR WOMEN'. For climate change the list of targets and slogans goes on and on and so do the possibilities of what you can write on your sash: 'NO NEW COAL', 'REFORM CLIMATE POLICY', 'NO AIRPORT EXPANSION', TRAINS NOT PLANES', 'CLIMATE CODE RED'. It's down to the individual action group to decide on their best slogan, but there is something that unites us. Those with immense influence keep telling us that they are dedicated to cutting their emissions and creating a sustainable future. Yet everything they do undermines the things they say. The call that will unite us all is 'DEEDS NOT WORDS!'.

HOW TO MAKE YOUR CLIMATE SUFFRAGETTE SASH.

- Go to your local charity shop and buy the largest red item that you can find.
- Cut it into strips, approximately 20cm by 120cm.
- Fix it onto your body with the curve on your right shoulder and the two loose ends under your left arm.
- Mark where you will write your slogan, so that it can be read from left to right.
- Use white paint and write your message.
- Sew or safety-pin the two loose ends.

HOW TO DO AN ACTION

A successful action should raise the profile of climate change: both the problems and the solutions. People will experience your action directly and hopefully they'll end up reading it in the local, or even national, press. Now's the time to reconnect with any community you've ever been part of. A strong network ensures a successful, supported and excited event. Once you've formed your local Climate Rush group, create a Facebook site and start discussing things online so that your face-to-face meetings can be really focused and effective. Once you've prepared the action to launch your group, organise a meeting with a local reporter. They might be interested in covering the fact that the Climate Suffragettes have come to town. Ask for advice on how to attract media attention. Maybe you can recruit her as a secret Suffragette! Talk to everyone you meet about climate change and the empowering example you set by your campaign.

HOW TO HAVE A SUCCESSFUL ACTION

1. Invite your local MP and any other local celebrities to come along.
2. Invite local press.
3. Invite everyone that you know and even more that you don't.
4. Encourage your Rushers to come in period dress, or at least wide-brimmed hats and sashes.
5. Invite the CEO of the company/industry that you are targeting.
6. Write a press release and send it to the local and national press
7. Make sure that you have good photos of the event.
8. Send a press release after the event including your pictures.
9. Send your picture for uploading onto the Climate Rush website.

MEDIA FOR AN ACTION

The media will amplify your message. Those of you who are interested in talking to the press should form a separate group which will deal with the PR. There are three questions that need to be at the heart of your strategy.

1. What's the action?
2. What's the headline?
3. What's the photo?

You need to write a press release ahead of the protest. Once the action has begun you should send the press release out to your media contacts and all of the local and national newsdesks. It's also worth chasing up journalists and asking them politely to cover the story. It's important to organise a photographer for the action. For most newspapers the photo makes the story and if it's a good enough shot they might publish it regardless of whether they consider your story news. If you've got someone who can film the event then beg them to take their footage, immediately after it's shot, down to your local broadcaster. If you're in London then go to Millbank, the television news studios.

PRESS RELEASES (PRs) INCLUDE:

Headline A sharp and engaging headline.

Paragraph 1 Three lines on what happened; just the facts of the story.

Paragraph 2 More on what happened – when it happened, how many were involved, why did they choose this target.

Paragraph 3 A statement from one of the people in the action explaining why they have taken the action that they have.

Paragraph 4 What has your action achieved? Can you find another point of view? Call the offices of your target and ask them to defend their actions.

Ends This is how you let the editor know that he or she has read to the end of your press release.

Notes to editor Include short biographies of those involved and a short biography of your action group, with its mandate and any research links to facts contained in your press release. Give a number to call for interviews, updates and media of the action (photos, film etc.). Use a dedicated press phone or SIM card so you won't get pestered by the press after the event.

Photo The photo of the action will be the thing that convinces a newspaper to print or not to print. Whilst designing the action think about the photo – what will it be of? Will it communicate your action? If the newspapers only printed the photo would it make clear what you were doing and why?

- Send the photo out with the PR with a snappy caption, which will act a bit like the headline.
- The person taking the photo or the film needs to be totally dedicated to getting that photo out of the action area and into the hands of the media. Once they've taken the photo they should get out of there – you don't want to risk the camera being confiscated or the photographer being arrested. They should get to an internet café or

a wireless hotspot, upload the photo and send it out to the press list, with the same title as the PR that has been sent out. Upload your footage onto the internet – youtube.com is probably the easiest to use – and send the link along with your photos.

- Call the contacts on your press list and make sure that they've received the PR and the photo. Ask them what they're going to do with it and use all your powers of persuasion to get them to run it. If the nationals aren't biting then concentrate on local or niche market papers.

- Once you've built up relationships with individual journalists, invite them to join you on actions. Tell them about it before it happens and offer them exclusivity. You can also publish your own news on www.indymedia.co.uk.

LEGAL CONSIDERATIONS FOR AN ACTION

Being part of a direct action group is a bit like the adult version of Scouts. There's only really one rule and everything else follows from that: *always be prepared.* The problem with direct action is that no matter how much preparation you do there will always be contingencies – moments when things are going wrong and you need to think on your feet. Some things will always catch you unawares, so it's important that for the areas that you can plan your action is as tight as possible. Most direct actions will not lead to arrest, especially if they are mass shows of civil disobedience. But inevitably, some will. If you want to make your point, be visible and have your voice heard, then you'll discover that you're treading a delicate line between the legal and illegal. A night in the nick is made bearable, almost enjoyable, if you know there are people awake on the outside watching your back. If you are going to do a direct action then the legal side is one area where you can never be too prepared.

1. Find out the laws you might be breaking.
2. Give your activists a briefing.
3. After their arrest follow them through their
   police-cell journey.
4. Meet them fresh from the cell with a hug,
   some food and cash for getting home.

Spend a couple of hours on the internet (or in the library looking at actual books if you prefer) and find out which laws you might break during your action. If you're making yourself immovable then it'll be 'aggravated trespass', if you're decommissioning a piece of carbon emitting machinery then it'll be 'criminal damage' and if you're anywhere near an airport then there'll be all sorts of sneaky by-laws to be aware of. Once you know the laws you can find out the worst case scenario for sentencing. But we aren't criminals and judges do tend to appreciate that fact. We've yet to see a climate activist get jail time. Tell your activists what they can expect from the strong-arm of the law, then reassure them – we're finding the courage to do what's right.

Whilst your team of activists is preparing for their action, you, the legal team, will be busy preparing hero-support. From the moment they're arrested your activists will be completely isolated from the real world and it's down to the legal team to be their connection to the outside world. Find out what police station they're in by calling round the closest police stations to the action. You should have the names and numbers of the activists' nearest and dearest (mums, dads, bosses, husbands, children etc.) who will need to know they've been arrested. Call those people and keep updating them throughout the day.

The legal hub needs to be completely secret. While you're guiding your friends through their cell experience and communicating with their solicitors and loved ones you shouldn't mention where you are and you should only use 'clean' phones – freshly bought, pay as you go, intended for this action only. If the police discover where you are then they could come and arrest you too, for the crime of 'conspiracy'. When the activists are arrested they should have your phone number written in indelible marker across their arm. Their one phone call from the station will be to you. They'll tell you which police station they're at (if you haven't managed to find them) and tell you what they've been arrested for, then it's your job to get solicitors involved with their case. Cheer them up by telling them about all the great press that your action has attracted. If they're in for a while then send someone down to the police station. There is really nothing better than coming out of a lonely cell and being greeted by a friend with enough money for a drink at the nearest pub and the train fare home.

FOR THE ACTIVISTS IN THE CELLS:

Just keep remembering that you have done it! You've completed the task you set yourself, news of your action is probably pinging its way around media outlets all over, and while you're locked up you should keep feeling proud of yourself. Don't talk to the police. They'll call you 'darling', wink at you and act super-friendly, but be careful – everything you say after the point of arrest is on the record and they'll be looking for something incriminating. If you give them your name, address and date of birth at the custody desk then it'll take them less time for them to identify you and they'll feel pleased that you've cooperated. Once they've got your arrest they might send someone round to search your house, so warn those you live with and clear your room of anything you'd prefer not to reach police hands.

In the cell you can finally get some sleep. It's not the Hilton, but there's a bed and eventually the extreme-sports buzz that you got from doing the action will die down. Try to get some rest. They can hold you for up to twenty-four hours without charge so ask if you can take a book in and try not to stress over the wasted hours.

At some point in those twenty-four hours they'll come and collect you for your interview. Be sure that you only answer 'no comment'. They'll want to waste your time and provoke you to say something, anything. Just keep your cool and stick to your one answer – 'no comment'. However much they're pissing you off I promise you're being far more aggravating by sticking to a 'no comment' interview.

If you've been wiling away your cell time, getting more and more annoyed by the focus of police attention, then this is your chance to give them as good as you've got. Always answer 'no comment'. This will protect you and the people who have been arrested alongside you. It will protect you from implicating yourself or others. It's a bond of trust between you and your fellow activist. Eventually you'll be let out. Your friends will be there waiting. Go and wind down at the nearest pub, café, restaurant or park then, exhausted, head home to bed.

ACTION PLANNING

TARGET: Your regional airport

If you live near one of the following airports then your area is under threat. The government has begun or is planning an expansion of your airport. In doing so they will dramatically increase your local pollution levels and global CO_2 emissions. Airports up for expansion are: Edinburgh, Glasgow International, Glasgow Prestwick, Aberdeen, Dundee, Inverness, Cardiff International, Belfast International, Manchester, Liverpool John Lennon,

Blackpool, Carlisle, Newcastle, Teesside International, Leeds-Bradford International, Birmingham International, East Midlands, Bristol International, Bournemouth International, Exeter International, Stansted, Heathrow, Gatwick and Luton.

DEMAND: No airport expansion. Trains not planes.

ACTION: Individual ...... **Take fewer flights.**
             Community .... **Stage a sit-in /**
                         Edwardian dinner party.

Having an Edwardian dinner party is easy and engaging. The first and most important thing is your invitation. Whether you're sending it out to your Facebook group or letter-dropping your community you need an invitation that captures the fun mood of the event.

Cordially invite your local environmental groups, mother and toddler groups, church groups etc. to converge in the main terminal of your regional airport at 8pm on your chosen date. Inform them that food will be shared, picnic style, and invite them to make picnic blankets emblazoned with their particular message or demand.

At 8pm try and organise a signal that will let your Climate Suffragettes know the dinner has begun. This could be the ringing of a bell, the first chords of some music or a simple shout that it is time to sit down for dinner. Roll out the picnic blankets, pass around fliers about aviation and the environment, open your baskets and begin.

The police will want to know when you plan to end your dinner. Just keep in mind that it is not illegal to eat dinner in an airport and end when you've all finished. Or stay indefinitely. You have the power and so the decision belongs to you.

EXAMPLE (organised in six weeks):

The Press Release

HUNDREDS OF CLIMATE SUFFRAGETTES STAGE SIT IN DINNER AT HEATHROW AIRPORT.

Hundreds of protesters from the environmental action group, 'Climate Rush', have staged a sit-in dinner at Heathrow Airport, Terminal One. The night before Labour decides whether to allow the construction of a third runway at Heathrow, these women and men have converged to demand an end to airport expansion.

Over 600 protesters, dressed in Edwardian outfits and wearing red 'Climate Rush' sashes, unfurled their picnic blankets (complete with embroidered protest slogans) at 7pm sharp. A string quartet signaled the beginning of their feast and played throughout their three hour occupation. Seventeen check-in desks were closed and over 90% of flights were diverted to other terminals.

Alice, a spokesperson for the group, said,

'We've come to Heathrow to let the government know that whatever tomorrow's decision, the third runway will not be built. Hundreds of normal, law-abiding people have come together, dressed as Suffragettes, to block the running of an entire terminal. Civil disobedience is growing and we will have our protest heard. I'm sick of government hypocrisy. We've got to cut emissions but expansion at Heathrow will make that impossible. So tonight we've transformed this airport into a space for creative community.'

If the expansion of Heathrow goes ahead then it will become the single biggest of emitter of CO_2 in the UK, ten thousand people will be displaced and an Anglo-Saxon village will be bulldozed. The Archbishop of Canterbury, the Mayor of London and the Conservative party have all come out against Heathrow's expansion.

Ends

Notes to editor:
Climate Rush is a non-violent direct action group
see www.climaterush.co.uk

Last year they organised a protest where 1,000 women stormed the

House of Commons. They threaten to escalate their civil disobedience if the government does not take comprehensive action to tackle climate change.

***

The real story

I was worried about this action. The police had been trying to get in touch with the Climate Rush group and the media had reported that we were anarchists, planning to close Heathrow Airport for a night or even longer. It was a cool suggestion but far beyond our real plans. We'd received a letter from BAA which had almost seemed like a threat:

> 'You should be aware that the planned protest coincides with a scheduled El Al departure during which armed Metropolitan Police officers will be patrolling the terminal. Given the current situation in the Middle East it is vital that protestors do not put themselves at risk within the terminal.'

I certainly didn't want to put anyone at risk and I was nervous that I'd be recognized by the police and turfed out of the airport before the picnic could begin. After leaking the story of police threats to *The Observer* I decided that the best way to avoid a preemptive arrest was to turn up to the airport in disguise. A friend of mine is a costume designer and make-up artist. He decided that for one night he could transform me into a bearded man. The afternoon of the protest I sat in his make-up chair whilst he laboriously stuck my beard on strand by strand. After two hours he spun me around and I faced the mirror. I burst out laughing. I looked like the stereo-typical image of a tramp – a very male tramp. I had a brown beard, a dirty scar above my eye and muck scraped onto my teeth. In the station, waiting for the train to Heathrow, I bought a newspaper and was surprised by the shop assistant saying, 'There you go, bruv.' The disguise had worked.

As I walked into the terminal I was worried about the police presence and also anxious that we wouldn't have many protesters. We'd posted on our site that people should come with their picnic, blankets and suffragette sash hidden in their carry-on bag, but I thought I'd recognize more people among the police and travellers. I sat in the pub above the departure gate which we hoped our protest would block, and drank the half of ale that seemed fitting for my disguise. Three police encircled me and asked me what I was doing there. Molly, my favourite police officer, was one of them. I spoke quietly, trying to make my voice sound husky, but Molly peered past my beard and dirty face and began to laugh.

'I can't believe it. Tamsin, don't you remember me?'

'Y'what? I dunno who you are,' I gruffed.

'Come on Tamsin, don't you recognize me? I arrested you outside Parliament.'

She almost seemed hurt that I had forgotten her, and realizing that the game was up I spoke normally.

'Of course I remember you. Uhmm, are you going to let us have our picnic…? And, I want to go to the loo and take this beard off.'

She smiled and nodded before escorting me to the loo.

After I'd taken off my facial hair it was almost time for the protest to begin. I was still unsure about the numbers. I recognized about forty people but that didn't seem enough, especially after all of the media hype about our planned occupation.

The string quartet, the signal that it was time to unfurl picnic blankets and remove disguises, struck up a chord. The music transformed the space. Suddenly, travellers were unpacking their carry-ons, rolling out blankets, sitting down and passing round food. Over 700 people ignored the bylaw that meant protesting in an airport was illegal and sat down for over three hours to listen to music, chant and dance. I loved it that my beard had gone. I could be myself, cheering and smiling and dancing up close to the police. At one point I was hoisted on someone's shoulders. I yelled and the whole space stomped their feet. The police looked bemused and left us to our party.

TARGET: Your local RBS-Natwest

The Royal Bank of Scotland, which owns NatWest, prides itself on being 'the oil and gas bank' – that's from their website! We're now their biggest shareholder. The British public owns approximately 70% of the largest financiers of the fossil fuel industry. The emissions caused by oil and gas projects within the RBS project finance plan to reached 36.9 million tonnes in 2005, which is equivalent to the emissions of 75% of the UK's homes. Provisional figures for 2006 show that RBS emissions were greater than the combined emissions of Scotland. The thirty oil and gas project finance deals signed between 2001 and 2006 lock in future emissions of 655 million tonnes over the next fifteen years, more than equivalent to the UK's entire annual emissions. Since we became shareholders they have been involved in financing loans to coal, oil and gas companies worth nearly £10 billion – over 50% of the amount that the bank has received from us.

DEMAND: Invest in a sustainable future
    (green technology and infrastructure).

ACTION: Individual .... **If you bank with RBS or NatWest then change banks.**
   Community .... **Stage a mock robbery at your local branch.**

Feeling theatrical...
If you're feeling theatrical then why not find some scraps of white lace, fold them into triangles and make Climate Suffragette balaclavas. Get in touch with the Robin Hood spirit, remind yourself of whose

money's being used to fund the fossil fuel industry (70% of it is your money) and whose future their investments put at risk. Be sure to let their CEO know that if he invests in environmentally sound industry you'll call the whole heist off. Take leaflets that detail their cowardly investments and include information on how best to switch to 'The Cooperative Bank'. As you 'rob' the bank ask your cronies to hand out leaflets to customers.

EXAMPLE (organised in three days)

The Press Release

CLIMATE RUSH LOCKS DOWN THE HEAD OFFICE OF THE ROYAL BANK OF SCOTLAND.

Sixty protesters, from the direct action 'Climate Rush', held a leaving party for Sir 'Fred the Shred' two days after he retired from RBS keeping his £703,000 pension. The group erupted outside the head office on Bishopsgate at 1pm and partied until 3pm. The protest group shared food and heard speeches which were amplified by a bike-powered sound system. After their meal the sound system played pop songs such as Abba's 'Money, Money, Money' and Madonna's 'Material Girl'. The protesters, dressed as bandits, danced around the bankers waiting to be allowed entrance into the building.

Chloe, spokesperson for the group, said:

'We can see whose side the state is on. Last week Fred Goodwin was allowed to walk away from a bank we've bailed out taking his £703,000 pension with him. Now the taxpayer has to foot the bill for a protest outside their bank. The Royal Bank of Scotland is largely owned by us and yet there are no regulations over where it spends our money. In a time of climate change it's the biggest financier of the fossil fuel industry. We shouldn't be using public money to fund runaway climate change.'

The protesters are calling for RBS to be publicly accountable. They ask that taxpayers money should be used to fund projects for the public good.

Ends

Notes to editor:
Climate Rush is a non-violent direct action group
see www.climaterush.co.uk

Its members have rushed Parliament, held a picnic at Heathrow Airport and disrupted the UK Coal Awards. They threaten to escalate their civil disobedience if the government does not take comprehensive action to tackle climate change.

***

The real story

I jumped off the train at Liverpool Street and made my way to the HQ of the Royal Bank of Scotland. It was surrounded by police and there were two more vans waiting further up the road. In front of the police was a bike powered sound-system and in front, a group of animated activists were dancing around. My friend Apoc was mincing around offering the policemen tea from his big copper pot. As he turned and danced.away I saw a policeman eye him up and down then shrug. I did the same and noticed that Apoc was wearing a dress. Two girls were dancing frantically together having thrown off their work jackets and undone their shoes. They jumped up next to a man in a suit and he smiled at them before nodding to the beat and saying, 'Well, it is incredible, £703,000 for the rest of his life. And what do we get?!'

***

TARGET: Your local Shell garage.

Although guilty of environmental damage throughout the world, Shell Oil is infamous for its exploitation of Nigerian oil reserves. As well as damaging the environment with frequent oil spills, it has destroyed villages by laying pipelines, polluted farmland and rivers and given the local people respiratory diseases. Shell makes over

$300 million a year from Nigeria and is about to begin work on a $4 billion natural gas venture together with the Nigerian government. This money will almost certainly only benefit the corrupt ruling elite, while the poor of Ogoni remain among the poorest in Africa, with no running water or electricity and inadequate schools and healthcare. The people have endured twenty-five years of military rule. Oil provides 90% of Nigeria's foreign income, and about half of this comes from Shell. In May 1994, after a secret meeting with Shell, the Nigerian Head of Internal Security called for 'ruthless military operations'. The result? Dozens of villages destroyed, thousands of people made homeless and hundreds massacred. Shell has even admitted that it supplied guns for these 'security operations'.

DEMAND: Stop exploiting the people whose oil you buy.
Use your profits to invest in a clean energy future.

ACTION: Individual ..... Drive less, get a bike, write
to Shell.

Community .... Organise a bike ride,
blockade your local garage.

Get your Climate Suffragette network together. Choose a date and time and organise to meet, in costume and with a bike, in your town centre. Ride through the streets (taking up as much of the road as you want) with skirts blowing in the wind and hat ribbons streaming. Make your way to the local Shell garage and chain your bikes across the entrance way. With no way to enter the garage you'll effectively have closed it for business. As ever, be sure to invite Shell's CEO. It's his business practice that has forced your blockade. Many petrol stations have a safety button to shut off all of the pumps in case of emergency. Perhaps you've made a banner that reads: 'CLIMATE EMERGENCY: CLOSED FOR BUSINESS'. If this isn't the perfect emergency to turn off the pumps then what could be?

EXAMPLE: THE BIKE RUSH

Press release

CLIMATE RUSH INTRODUCES PEDAL POWER

Hundreds of environmental campaigners and keen cyclists will take to the streets of London on June 1st to call for no new coal fired power stations and tougher environmental measures to control CO2 emissions.

Pedal Power, a bike ride organised by the Climate Rush aims to give the Secretary of State Energy and Climate Change Ed Miliband, a taste of the civil disobedience he can expect if real climate justice fails to materialise.

June 1st sees Parliament return from recess for the summer sitting. On the same evening a UK coal conference will be taking place at Chatham House, with all the key players in the coal world present.

The bike rush will begin right outside the conference making its presence known, before winding its way through town, embarking on a tour of companies who put their desire for profits before the genuine needs of the inhabitants of our planet.

A Climate Rush spokesperson said:

'If we are to keep global temperature rises around or below 2°C we must stop building new coal fired power stations, start investing in low carbon energy alternatives and reduce our reliance on fossil fuels through more homes and buildings insulation, less consumerism and a turn-around in attitudes to transport: trains not planes, bikes not cars.

We will not stop our non-violent but highly disruptive campaign of activities until politicians and energy companies stop polluting our world and its inhabitants into oblivion.'

In true Climate Rush style the bike ride will end with a picnic, with blankets and food and drink to share.

Ends

Notes to editor:

Climate Rush is a non-violent direct action group
(see http://www.climaterush.co.uk)

- Climate Rush is a broad coalition of people, all of whom believe
  that drastic action is needed to halt Climate Change. They will
  pressure the UK government until their demands are met.
- Coal is responsible for 50% of the climate change gases in the
  atmosphere caused by human activity.

***

The real story

The day before the Bike Rush, twenty climate rushers came to my
house for one of our 'creative days'. We wanted this to be our most
beautiful protest yet – the weather forecast was for clear sunshine
and we knew we were in for an amazing bike ride through the heart
of London. We screen-printed over 400 sashes with a new slogan,
'PEDAL POWER', and then made fifty bright red Climate Rush
flags which we planned to give to fifty lucky punters to stick on the
back of their bikes. That creative day, and the protest itself, were
followed by no less than three film crews – documentary makers
were becoming more and more excited by our particular brand of
protest! We were all really excited, especially as this was the first rush

were we had a kind of uniform: red and white striped bloomers that one of our rushers had run up on a sewing machine.

As we arrived at Chatham House on the day itself there was the usual mix of nerves and anticipation. Would anyone turn up? Would they want a PEDAL POWER sash? Would we be able to keep everyone safe through the rush-hour-trafficked streets of London?

We'd scheduled an hour to converge, and soon the trickle of people arriving became a flood – so many people that the police, who'd been trying to blockade us, had to give up and let us overflow into the road. Just as we were about to set off, a trailer arrived being pulled by two Hare Krishna monks on bikes. They were feeling the strain as their trailers contained two banjo players, a man with a drum kit, and a Red Jen from the Belle Stars (a rock group from the 80s) singing her heart out. It was the perfect signal for the start of the ride. We circled St James's square and then headed into the centre of town, being joined by more and more cyclists; about 600 by the time we hit Oxford Street. Passers-by just didn't know what to make of us. A guy on a tandem with a pedal-power sound-system kept the gawping crowd up to speed with what they were seeing: 'This is the Climate Rush pedal-powered protest, demanding no new coal so we can save the planet for future generations.'

As we headed through the heart of London's shopping district, I heard a cyclist up ahead giving a different sort of message. He was using a megaphone and shouting abuse at the people on the street:

'Stop shopping you mindless idiots!' I raced up to him and begged him to be quiet – yes, consumerism is a problem, but telling people what to do like that would just make them switch off and ignore us. I don't know if he agreed with me but at least he stopped shouting.

Two hours later and we were sitting on Westminster Bridge, having closed the road for our picnic. People danced to the music booming out of bike-powered sound-systems and there was a really joyful atmosphere. Tourists stopped to take photographs as we celebrated in the shadow of Big Ben and the Houses of Parliament. We'd hung a huge banner saying 'Remember, Remember the 5th of December!' down the side of the bridge so that the MPs having tea out on the terrace could see our message. Two rushers even climbed up on the statue of Queen Boudicea and rode her horses wearing their Climate Rush sashes. Nobody was arrested even though we were obstructing a highway and holding an unauthorised protest near Parliament.

Eventually the police told us if we didn't leave then riot police would be brought in to move us on. At that point we all decided it was time to head for a pub, where we stayed until closing time, talking to the strangers who'd made it their first Climate Rush protest and locals wanting to know where we got our bloomers.

The following day the police statement in the *Evening Standard* said that they had allowed us to close the bridge as using force to remove us would have been 'disproportionate when viewed against the behaviour, mood and make-up of the crowd'. Once again our polite and civilised form of protest completely blind-sided police protocol!

***

TARGET: A Suffragette Anniversary

We take inspiration from the Suffragettes, so what better way to show our gratitude than by celebrating a centenary? For over five years they mounted action after action, so there are loads of anniversaries to work with. The first Climate Rush was the centenary celebration of their Suffragette Rush. Six months on and the centenary of Marjory Humes' action came up. It was also four days since Ed Miliband had declared his plan to invest in a new generation of coal-fired power stations, his answer to our energy insecurity. So what did the Rushers do? They glued themselves round the same statue and spent two hours in the heart of Parliament talking about the need for truly clean energy.

'Marjory Humes chained herself to this statue, one hundred years ago today, because the people in this building were not listening. Well, a hundred years later and I think that this government is in need of a wake up call.

Climate change is the biggest threat to humanity, and it's not happening in fifty years, it's not happening in ten years, it is happening now. 300,000 people a year are already dying from diseases spread by rising temperatures. NASA scientists think that the Arctic sea ice could be gone as early as next summer. And what is our government doing? Proposing airport expansion, green-lighting the third runway and now bringing in a new generation of coal-fired power stations using unproven CCS technology.

If we build coal-fired power stations we will use coal-fired power stations, regardless of whether we can safely deal with their emissions. How can we expect China and India to take us seriously in international climate talks when our policies back home show we have as much intention of respecting large emissions cuts as we have of meeting our targets for 2012? This is a government that talks climate change and then shows those words to be empty in everything it does. In the spirit of the Suffragettes we need action rather than speechifying, and deeds not words.

DEEDS NOT WORDS.'

LOCAL GOVERNMENT: 'What can a council do to tackle climate change?' Alexis Rowell, Liberal Democrat councillor for Camden

At the centre of the transformation of your community lies your local government. They are ploughing funds and time into climate change solutions. They've got to. The central government has signed up to 8% cuts in our CO_2 emissions by 2050. It will be impossible for them to deliver this at a national level and so they've passed the buck and are looking to local governments for results. There are simple actions that don't need to involve the council. You needn't lobby them to organise a swap-shop day. Set one up yourself. You don't need your local government to set up allotments. Use local green spaces and launch some community planting. Your local council is far more likely to fund a project that is already up and running rather than create something from scratch. With the credibility gained in their own area, local MPs will be able to go to Westminster and prove that there is a public mandate for tackling climate change.

ENERGY EFFICIENT HOUSING

The opportunity? With proper insulation we could achieve a 20% cut in the UK's carbon dioxide emissions. Energy efficient housing would also be cost-efficient.

The solution?

- Free cavity wall and roof insulation for all.
- Offer loans for solid wall insulation and double glazing paid back out of energy bill saving.
- Switch to a green energy provider and encourage your community to follow suit.
- Install heating controls and meters in housing estates.

WASTE AND RECYCLING

The opportunity?

In the UK we recycle approximately 20% of our waste yet in Austria (and other EU countries) they recycle over 60%. In the middle of the Pacific floats a garbage dump around twice the size of Texas. We are running out of room to hide our waste.

The solution?

- Buy less.
- Reuse your plastic bags and boycott packaged food and bottled water.
- Introduce swap shops, street swap days and a reuse/swap website.
- Improve access to recycling and create more on-street recycling centres.
- Compost your food. Waste food makes up around 30% of household waste but it could be a resource for your garden. Your council will provide compost bins and deliver them to your door, if you ask.

TRANSPORT

The opportunity?

Fewer cars would immediately improve our environment. Our streets would be safer, the air would be cleaner and it would be far more enjoyable to go outside on a summer's day. In London the mayor is planning to introduce a free bike scheme. These schemes could be exported across the UK's councils.

The solution?

- Buy a bicycle and encourage your friends to do the same. Nothing will make the streets safer for cyclists than more bicycles.
- More pedestrian friendly streets and properly separated bike-lanes.
- Car clubs, electric cars and free bike schemes.
- Introduce emissions-based parking permits.

FOOD

The opportunity?

The average vegetarian diet saves approximately 605 litres of crude oil per year. A vegan diet would save 950 litres. Sourcing our food locally would hugely reduce our emissions as so much of our food is flown into the country. Bought food is more expensive than home grown. It also doesn't offer you any security over your food source.

The solution?

- Encourage the growth of food on every balcony, in every garden and on every hard surface.
- Introduce farmers markets into your local community.
- Share meals to reduce waste.
- Generate electricity or vehicle fuel (biomethane) from food waste.

These small actions are not revolutionary, but if implemented on a large enough scale they would completely change our lives. It would not be a violent uprising. It would begin in our daily choices, graduate to our streets and soon be reflected in central government policy.

***

You can find Climate Suffragettes in your family, faith group, book club, local parents, colleague or your friends in the pub. Time is running short and we need to take the initiative and instigate change.

Step One is shaping community decisions.

Step Two is changing decisions as consumers and in the workplace.

Step Three is influencing government and industry. Start with something small and see how far you can go. We all know that spirit of defiance which comes when we stumble across something that just isn't fair. We can win this fight, but only if we stand together. We will be one part of one network, united under a national banner.

Our cry will be 'DEEDS NOT WORDS!'.

In the new year we will make our presence felt as the MPs gear up for a general election but this year we need to take a stand. On the first Saturday in December, a march will encircle Parliament to demand climate action. This will be our final chance to make an impact on our government's contribution to the UN Climate Summit in Copenhagen in December 2009. The Kyoto Protocol – an international agreement committing 184 parties to the prevention of climate change and global warming – runs out in 2012. The Copenhagen conference will be the first time that the parties of the UNFCCC (United Nations Framework Convention on Climate Change) will be laying out specific details for the kind of climate agreement that will replace it. Governmental representatives from 200 countries could agree to do something meaningful, radical and legally binding. It is vital that our government hears our call for change in the run up to this significant event.

We have seen these marches before and we have felt our power robbed as the government ignores our demands. We don't have time to wait for another international meeting. Big decisions and big commitments must be made at Copenhagen. If we want our government to take note of our protest we need to do more than just march, we need to Rush. The march will take place on December 5th and will end next to Big Ben at 3pm. Then it's time for you to make history. Rush into Parliament with us and have our message sent throughout the world. We will hold our leaders to account and we will demand climate justice. The time for words is over. The time for action is now.

CHAPTER SEVEN

ON THURSDAY 2ND APRIL 2009 THE G20 CAME TO LONDON, on a mission to sort out the economic crisis. By the end of their visit the twenty richest nations had agreed that $1.1 trillion could be whipped from nowhere and injected back into the global economy, Berlusconi had got a scolding from the Queen for his overloud voice and Ian Tomlinson had been killed when a policeman beat him to the ground.

Gordon Brown prepared himself for the G20 talks by flying to conference rooms the world over and saying big things about responding to the recession with a lot more spending. Protest groups of every shape and size geared up for the G20 talks planning to converge on the City of London. The police and press thought this would mean a big smash, grab and hang approach. Certain protest groups thought it meant storming the Bank of England. As for

Climate Camp, they decided to set up a camp for twenty-four hours on Bishopsgate, the street that runs through the City of London.

⧗ TIME BOMB *Our global village*

Not everyone feels so strongly about climate change, even when they understand the science. Some people, like Danish academic and environmental writer Bjorn Lomborg, think that getting the third world out of poverty should be our number one priority. Others worry that the situation in the Middle East is about to explode. I agree that there are other things that are important, but I think that climate change should be top of the agenda – every agenda – because it is going to make every other problem SO much worse. If you think that Africa has food insecurity now, wait until the droughts that global warming will cause. If you think the Middle East is a hot spot now, wait until Israel is battling with its neighbours over fresh water. Rice crops decline 10% for every 1°C temperature rise. For half the world it makes up 80% of their food. As the climate changes first they'll stop exporting it, then they'll starve. I don't think we'll be eating much rice in Britain in ten years time.

Global warming is a global problem. It is going to affect every single person on earth and any feasible solution will have to involve everyone. Even though our global institutions have failed to stop climate change so far they are still our best and only hope. That's why Copenhagen in December 2009 is so important. That's when the countries of the world make decisions about what is going to replace the Kyoto Protocol when it runs out in 2012.

The Kyoto Protocol, the first international agreement on reducing carbon emissions, is generally thought to have been a failure. It took years to be agreed on, major world powers including America didn't even sign up to it and now it looks like everyone who did is going to miss their targets for emission cuts anyway. But it was significant – not least for demonstrating on an international stage the desire for change – and it established a precedent that we can build on. Some people want to give up on the international process of negotiation concerning climate change. I agree that so far it's been pretty ineffective. I agree that the way we negotiate gives too much power to the countries who are already rich, and that carbon trading schemes have handed huge amounts of cash to polluters. I know that climate change requires action according to a really fast timetable, possibly faster than international consensus can manage. But turning away from the international community isn't any more likely to solve the problem.

I'm not an economist, a politician or a scientist. I don't have any amazing or original ideas for dealing with this. But that's okay because there are some really really clever people who do. Here are a couple of their ideas that I think might just work.

Nicholas Stern – Global Green Recovery

Nicholas Stern, economist and academic, says we have three problems on our hands: poverty, climate change and the economic crisis. They are linked and cannot be thought about or tackled separately.

'We will not overcome world poverty unless we manage climate change successfully. I've spent my life as a development economist, and it's crystal clear that we succeed or fail on winning the battle against world poverty and managing climate change together. If we fail on one, we fail on the other.'

He wants huge amounts of green investment as a way of kick-starting the world economy and creating wealth. Among other things, he wants investment in clean technologies, loads more money in research and development and a massive upgrade of infrastructure. He also has a lot of political influence in the UK and the EU, and because he talks about using existing structures rather than making completely new ones they could be implemented by the G20 (or any individual country) immediately rather than having to wait for international consensus.

Oliver Tickell – Kyoto 2

Oliver Tickell – author, journalist and campaigner for health and environmental concerns – has the idea that carbon trading can work, if we charge people at the source (so at the coal mine or the oil rig), have lots of improved legislation to close up loopholes and keep a really clear idea of what the money raised is going to be used for. Basically there would be a set number of 'carbon permits' available each year, continually decreasing, which would be sold to companies or governments who are going to emit carbon. The price would rise as the number of permits was reduced, raising a steady $1 trillion a year. About half of Tickell's book *Kyoto2: How to Manage the Global Greenhouse* (2008), discusses what this money should be spent on, such as paying to preserve rainforests, spreading low-carbon technologies, helping poor countries adapt to climate change and relocating millions of climate migrants. Most of the money would come from rich countries and be spent in poor countries. He thinks that the market is the best way forward, so long as it is heavily regulated.

Tradable Energy Quotas – David Fleming

TEQs are an idea my housemate's boss, David Fleming, came up with. This involves a kind of energy rationing which covers a nation's whole economy. A TEQ unit is a certain amount of CO_2 produced by a product – so coal, which is the dirtiest fuel, would use more TEQ units than natural gas. Every person in the country would get a certain number of these units for free every year, while organisations, companies and governments would have to buy the units they need at auction. There would only be a certain number of permits available and this would get smaller every year. Individuals would only need to use their units when they buy energy directly – for everything else the carbon price would be included in the overall price of the item. So food which didn't use oil-driven tractors would end up being less expensive than food which did, for example. People who live really low-carbon lifestyles can sell their spare permits and as poor people use less energy than rich people it could help create more equality. And everyone would have to think creatively and work together to reduce their carbon footprints: businesses, grass-roots initiatives and governments, all using the same system, thinking about carbon on a day-to-day basis and finding common solutions.

Ecoequity and Stockholm Environmental Institute – Greenhouse Development Rights

These guys put poverty at the centre of a sustainable solution to climate change. They say we should have a 'development threshold', a level of income that determines whether you are responsible for paying for climate change. If you are below that level you'll be supported by richer people until you achieve it, and if you go over it then you start paying for people poorer than yourself. It wouldn't be anything like the level of consumption of the richest nations, but it would be a lot better than the current levels of poverty experienced by the third of people in the world currently living on $2 a day. By thinking in terms of individuals instead of nations they emphasise that richer people in the global south also need to take responsibility.

So far the only method we've found to make ourselves richer is to burn lots and lots of carbon. Some people think that stopping poor countries from producing emissions means condemning them to poverty. But I think that we need more imagination about what 'development' means, what other countries should be developing into and where we're heading ourselves. We're facing the most enormous crisis on earth. Some will say that it's hopeless, that we'll never be able to work together or make the changes we need. Sometimes, when I feel overwhelmed by everything, I think perhaps they're right. But I take comfort in the idea that this has never happened before. This is a completely unique problem. We have never had so much knowledge about what the future may entail, or had so many solutions. And if Nicholas Stern is right then this challenge is also a huge opportunity to achieve justice in a world which so desperately needs it. I guess this is the moment we've been waiting for, when the only option is to do the right thing.

I got the train to London the evening before the G20 protesters took to the streets. There'd been an email on an activist mail-out telling people to come to a meeting in Russell Square if they hadn't yet sorted out a plan. Sitting round in a circle in the middle of the square I felt how distant I had become from the activist scene. Following the previous Climate Rush event, I'd disappeared for a month or so to remove myself from the media spotlight, and to put some distance between me and the negative opinions of the activist world. There'd been some hostility at my media-friendly antics and I wondered whether the bridges between me and the movement were too badly burned to be rebuilt.

During the meeting Chloe, the girl sitting on my right, was my saving grace. She was the one person who would properly meet my eye, and she even gave me the odd ironic smile. Before the meeting she'd asked me why she kept seeing my face in the paper. She'd questioned my motives a bit, but she also seemed to believe that my heart was in the right place, and maybe my strategy too. She's part of the Climate Rush now, a facilitator in our Bristol crew.

***

I woke at 7am, half an hour before the alarm. It felt a bit like Christmas, this day when London would be overrun with protestors. As Obama was crossing London for the G20 'Leader's Breakfast' I stood in my pyjamas stirring raisins into my porridge. I wondered whether he would hear about the protests. Amongst the reports of rioting anarchists and police brutality I hoped he would hear something about the Climate Camp, and that he'd be inspired by the people-power of our peaceful occupation of Bishopsgate, the main artery of our financial district and the site of the Carbon Trading Exchange.

With bunting in my bag and the church clock chiming noon, I sat on the steps of Spitalfield's market in East London waiting for Chloe. We were supposed to make our way to the camp together. We'd arrive at 12.30pm on the dot and then unpack our camp stuff, hopefully surrounded by thousands of other campers. On our way over we were very covert, watching each other's backs, looking out for the police and other obstructions. We'd been expecting it to be near impossible to reach Bishopsgate, but in fact the police presence we'd been told to expect was, at this point, just hype. At 12:30pm as scheduled we arrived on the street and were soon surrounded by people making lines of bikes and throwing open pop-up tents. This was the Climate Camp 'swoop'. It was a critical mass action. If there were enough people taking part then there'd be no way for the police to put an end to it. Within an hour over 2,000 people had joined the camp. The police didn't stand a chance.

I'd read the papers the day before and it had been the same story on every front page. This was my third Climate Camp and I'd got used to the false reports of secret anarchist plans. For the Climate Camp at Heathrow we'd had plans to board planes and threaten passengers, for the Camp at Kingsnorth coal-fired power station the police had found knives in bushes, and now, in the City, there were stories of the violence that we would do to the bankers. I knew just to shrug this off but it was a pity – I wondered how many other people with good reason to protest about the G20 would be put off by this media hype. Standing next to a traffic light as some kid climbed up it to hang a banner, I got a call from the *Evening Standard*. A journalist there told me he wanted me to write a diary of the day.

'I think my editor will publish it, if you can make it entertaining. Give us a bit of the inside story, how it got planned, what you hope it will achieve, worries about violence, that sort of thing.'

I was hesitant. I didn't want to speak on behalf of the movement – after all that had been my reason for getting out of town.

'Can't you get in touch with someone from the Camp? Someone who's been involved with all of the planning, someone who's a bit more clued up than me?'

He dismissed the idea, 'Tamsin, it has to be you, otherwise he won't print it. You know what it's about. We can trust you to find the right tone and our readers will know who you are and trust your point of view. We don't want polemic – just the story, what's going on and being said and thought behind the scenes.'

He wanted me to be able to write something that could actually make it past his editor and into the paper. He couldn't care less about the movement's politics. He just knew that if he pitched it just right he might be able to find a story from the other side of the protest.

'I just don't know... It will piss a lot of people off if they read the *Standard* and it's my voice describing all of this. I didn't help organise it.'

'But if it isn't your voice then there won't be anyone else's. This is your chance to explain to London the protesters' side.'

I was grateful for his interest. Since I appeared on the protest scene two years ago, Ian has been using me as an angle to write about climate change. He was the first journalist to become a friend. We have an understanding. If there's a protest coming up which I want to hit the papers, he'll try and find the angle that will get it into print. Sometimes this will mean focusing on my 'celebrity' status, sometimes it'll mean focusing on the anarchic element of an event, but, as he said after a particularly inflammatory piece he wrote: 'Look Tamsin, I'm sorry if you don't like the angle but in the end I've just given you a free advert. It might say you're a bunch of eco-terrorists but it's also got the time, date and place of the protest. And the name of your group. If people are interested they'll look you up and with a readership of 100,000 that's a pretty good thing.'

This time I didn't accept his offer. I wanted to, agreeing with him that it would be a great way to counter the stories of anarchy that was turning so many people off, but I didn't want to feel even more distant from my friends in the movement who seemed to have lost their faith in me.

***

The traffic had been stopped and more lone protesters were climbing lampposts, traffic lights, bus stops and buildings to hang their bunting. Banners had gone up at either end of the street: 'NATURE DOESN'T DO BAIL-OUTS'. People were walking in and out of the occupied street and there was a carnival atmosphere. I hoisted myself on top of a bus stop to get a better view. A bike-powered sound-system pumped out reggae just below so I stood up and danced precariously with seven or so protesters, vaguely wondering how much weight the bus stop top would hold (though the reggae was so loud these thoughts of health and safety were fairly easy to ignore…). There were tents as far as I could see and at each end of the camp stood a thin line of police. It looked as though we'd been more or less left to it.

By 3pm it was time for the first workshop. I climbed down and grabbed some food before joining Workshop Space 3 ('Fossil Fuel Economy – how the banks drive climate change'). There were three workshop spaces and printed programs were being passed around the camp. The camp wasn't just a protest or a celebration of people-power. It was also a resource, providing those who had come with a lot of information, as well as speeches and debates about why we'd chosen to camp that day outside the Carbon Trading Stock Exchange.

In the office windows looking down on the camp business men and women were standing, noses pressed against the glass, wearing their 'home-clothes' and waving wads of cash. Their faces were smug and self-satisfied. I pointed them out to Georgi, who had come with me, and her two friends. They laughed and told me not to stress. They weren't taking the protest that seriously. For them, and for quite a few of the 2,000 present, it was a mini-festival, the perfect place to while away a hot spring afternoon. They loved the spectacle of it all, and for one afternoon they'd feel involved, maybe even a little radicalized. But they weren't here because they got climate change, they'd come because Georgi had said it would be fun. I wondered if it mattered, if it was enough that they were here to make up numbers. One of them talked about the trip she was taking to New York the next weekend. I wondered if it was possible for this kind of event to be an entrance point into different sort of actions, different sorts of decisions.

I was caught up in these thoughts when someone from *Vogue* called me. They were stuck by the Bank of England and weren't being allowed out from behind the police lines. By the time their editor had barked an order at the police and got them out they were in a foul mood. I went to meet the deputy-editor and she immediately began bossing me about. She was so stylish that I couldn't do anything but obey. She wanted the prettiest protesters for a series of action shots and portraits. I felt compromised but as I looked at her tottering on her impractical shoes I still hoped that it might, just might, be the first step of many into our world.

***

I left the photo shoot and wandered off through the camp. A girl and a guy were making a lot of noise, engaging passers-by with their version of the children's game 'hangman':

'ROLL UP, ROLL UP,' called the girl, 'GUESS A LETTER AND WATCH THE BANKERS HANG!' They were both dressed in tailcoats and top-hats, their upper-lips sported mock moustaches. The guy held a sign which read, in blood red lettering, 'HANG A BANKER'. They were chatting to some passers-by and getting them to guess letter after letter. With each guess the girl drew the hapless banker in chalk on the pavement. The letters they had so far were:

S U _ - _ R I _ E

The banker wasn't doing so well – in two legs' time he'd be hanged.

A girl called to them from across the street, 'Hey, stop that, there's media around, we can't be hanging bankers.'

The boy laughed, 'What not even chalk-drawn bankers?'

The girl across the street rolled her eyes, 'Just pack it up, please,' and walked away. One of the on-lookers suddenly guessed 'SUB-PRIME!' and the group cheered.

The G20 excited plenty of protesters other than the Climate Campers. The media had focused on the most controversial players, and had had a field day in the pre-protest coverage with a group that called itself 'The Government of the Dead'. This group did very little for the inclusive press strategy of the Climate Camp, and – since to the media the various groups protesting against the G20 were largely indistinguishable – 'The Government of the Dead' had got us some terrible coverage. Led by a nutty professor from the University of East London, this group gave the media a message that they could really sink their teeth into. A message that would confirm to their public that joining the protesters as we took to the streets of London would mean joining up with a lynch mob.

This is what the old professor said during his fifteen minutes of fame: 'We are going to be hanging a lot of people like "Fred the Shred" from lampposts, and I can only say let's hope they are just effigies. If he winds us up any more I'm afraid there will be real bankers hanging from lampposts.'

This message was then transmitted to the entire nation on the front page of every paper, and so the peaceful and celebratory camp was somewhat eclipsed by the anarchic promise of 'The Government of the Dead'. Which was a pity, because it would have been really cool if before the summit, the coverage had been about climate change, the economic routine that fuels climate change, the impressive grass roots organization that can put together a campsite on one of the busiest streets in central London. I guess that's why the camper was telling the 'chalkers' off. She didn't want to fuel the media with more stories about weird protesters and their murderous messages.

We'd been hearing reports about what was going on at the Bank of England so I grabbed my friend Deborah and went down to take a look. Deborah had got back from travelling the month before, having completely freaked out about the environment and realised that she had to come home immediately (overland) and become an activist. Ten days after being in the Mauritanian Sahara she was locked on next to me on the gates of Parliament. Now she was experiencing her first Climate Camp. As we walked past the police lines I noticed my favourite policewoman, Molly. Her eye caught mine and she began to wave. Seems she's at every protest I go to. I went up to her and because I was buzzing from the energy of the camp I tried to give her a hug, but she was on duty and so she shrugged me off. I winked, she winked back and I walked off down to Bank.

The whole area was completely shut down. The protesters were caught behind fierce police lines and that was where they had to stay until the police decided it was time to let them go. There was nothing to see and I missed the relaxed atmosphere of the camp. Here there was too much aggression and an air of irritability and tension.

I arrived back in the camp and caught the perfect vision of all we were trying to achieve. Three girls were dancing on the roof of the police van. It was incredibly beautiful − the street was taken and the human spirit was dancing all over the old power system. Part of me wanted to hike myself up and join the dance with them but I knew these girls and I knew they'd be annoyed if I went and joined them in the spotlight.

Their dancing was written up in *The Times* the following day. A.A.Gill described it with his characteristic acerbic wit. While half the media was talking about rioters and broken bank windows he took a different slant. He'd had his face painted by a girl who'd taken the day off to join in the protest. She was a sweet sixteen-year-old called Paris and she provided him with the perfect angle to take the piss. She didn't have all the facts on carbon trading, and he assumed she was only there to have a laugh. Instead of writing about the thousands of protesters who had set up the camp because they wanted to put climate change on the G20 agenda, he wrote about young people who couldn't answer his questions with sound-bites about the business-as-usual international policy. All they talked about was the great time that they were having, and he wrote this up as a protest that he found difficult to take seriously.

The day wore on and eventually the office workers and journalists left. The sun had set and the day-trippers were going home, leaving those of us dedicated to a night on the streets to hold the fort. The police were now free to clear the camp without the scrutiny of the media or other onlookers.

I was somewhere in the middle of it all when shouts went up and suddenly everyone around me was sitting down. It happened really fast – all of a sudden we were sitting on the floor and surrounded by police, with hundreds of pairs of eyes darting over us from behind the policemen's shields. The air became tense and no-one moved in either direction. By sitting down we hoped that the only way forward for the police would be to trample over us. The police shouted at us to move back but no-one moved. We'd said that we would hold this street, in protest, for twenty-four hours. There were at least eleven hours still to go.

We were sat ten people thick, with maybe one hundred people stood further back, supporting those on the ground. There was no path forward for the police and they were hesitant to stomp over sitting bodies. Instead they began to pick off the front line. The first incident was immediately shocking: three riot-gear clad policemen put down their shields and grabbed an arm, a leg, the body of a sitting protester. A tug of war began. On one side you had the boys in blue and on the other the sitting protesters. More police got their batons out and hit the arms of those who were trying to hold tight to their buddy. The second any protestor's grip relaxed they were hauled behind the police-lines and that was it – they were gone from sight.

Protester-by-protester the police worked their way in. First the front line gone, then the second, third, fourth. People started to stand up with raised arms, shouting at the cops to go away, leave us alone, this was not a riot. And still more protesters were dragged from the scene, taken behind police-lines. No-one could see what was happening on that side, but everyone felt that their turn was coming fast. Should we have stood up and run away, or continued to sit on the ground while they battered and separated us?

There was a boy in a wheelchair who'd been at the back of the sitting protesters. The police-line came closer to him. I wondered what they'd do when it was his turn to be dragged out.

Soon everyone was standing with arms raised allowing the police to push us, so our feet would move. They charged. They screamed at us: 'MOVE BACK'. Those who didn't move fast enough were knocked to the floor by a policeman's shield and then hit down hard with a stick. All of us inched back but it wasn't fast enough for them. They charged and pushed and knocked us over, hit us back. I saw the boy on the floor, his wheelchair upturned. The police marched relentlessly on, it was their turn to swoop. They continued to push us from our site. Tripping up over the tents that we never had the chance to pack away, trampling over the sustainable workshop spaces, the farmer's market and the turf that someone had brought to the camp, yet we still weren't moving fast enough for them. They charged and more of us were pushed to the ground.

I shouted at them to slow down – we're leaving, you've won and you don't need to beat us out of here. A shield smacked me across my chest and I sprawled on the floor. I looked up and saw the visor of a helmet. An arm, clad in a yellow reflective jacket and holding a baton, was raised above me and then brought down onto my thigh. It happened again. And then again. And then again. A boy dragged me to my feet, shoved the policeman back and shouted, 'HOW DARE YOU DO THAT TO A GIRL?' His answer was a shield's edge jabbed into his face. I grabbed his arm, turned and we sprinted away. We all ran off. In less than five minutes they had cleared the street. No more protest. Camp was over.

As I walked, head down, back to my bike I could already feel the baton-shaped bruise rising on my thigh. It all felt so pointless and broken. I wanted to run into someone I knew but I didn't recognize the faces of the people coming from the camp. And then, as I drew closer to my bike, I saw Charlie fixing a note round my handlebars. I called to him. He turned, smiled, laughed, then ran to me. I wiped the tears from my face and he hugged me tight. He tore off his note and passed it to me with a grin. 'We've gone to Russell Square. There's music and rum. Get there quick. Cx.' I unlocked my bike and followed him as he rode off in that direction.

It took some days for the media to get to grips with this story of police brutality. Towards the end of the week footage from phones and cameras was filtering its way into journalists' hands. Shortly afterwards every major paper was splashed with stories about the latest report of police misconduct, the news that the cops had seriously abused their position and made use of any opportunity to bash a hippy. At the camp we had been trying to draw the media's attention to climate change, the crisis that is going to follow quick on the heels of our economic downturn. Instead the stories had been of rioting anarchists, saccharine students and police brutality. If the camp had been allowed its twenty-four hours then there would have been another story the following day, a story about the dedication of climate activists to have their message heard. But it wasn't to be. We've got a huge struggle ahead and the police are doing all they can to silence it. They stopped the protest that night and then they dominated the headlines for the following days. There were very few reports of what the Climate Camp had set out to achieve.

***

It wasn't a small circle in Russell Square. We jumped the fence and sat down with about forty other people. People drummed on empty Tupperware bowls, chinked bottles together and sang protest songs. There were faces round the circle that I recognised and I was sure they'd be annoyed to see me here as they were the people who'd been so pissed off with my courting the media. It was weird sitting with them after I'd spent most of the day trying to avoid them. Stranger still were the smiles they shot my way. My choices might be ones they'd never make, but ultimately we were still part of the same circle and we were still relieved to see each other, a little bruised but generally all right.

'What about the baked potatoes?'

'They needed way more time on that fire.'

'They couldn't have stopped the swoop. Campers everywhere and not enough police in the world to keep our tents in our bags.'

'Did you hear that some guy died outside the Bank of England?'

'Those fucking bankers waving their money at us.'

'Hey, pass the rum.'

I leant back. I was no longer in London. I was in some distant and uncertain place. But there was one constant truth, the voices I could hear around me and their hope. My vision was framed by trees, the haze of city lights, and beyond that stretched the sky.

ENDNOTES

CHAPTER 1

'I remember the sun shining, getting a good tan and being wound up by The God Delusion.'
Richard Dawkins, *The God Delusion* (Houghton Mifflin Harcourt, 2006)

'If flying is the most carbon intensive thing that I can do, it's important for me, waking up to climate change, to give that up.'
See www.eci.ox.ac.uk/research/ energy/downloads/predictanddecide. pdf for Dr Sally Cairns's and Carey Newson's article, 'Predict and Decide: Aviation, climate change and UK policy,' Environmental Change Institute, Oxford University, 2006.

'On the floor of my sitting room, I read about a 2°C rise in world temperatures. This is what the International Panel on Climate Change decided might be a 'safe' level of global warming, back in the early 1990s.'
In 1989 the UNEP Advisory Group said a 2°C rise is 'an upper limit beyond which the risks of grave damage to ecosystems,

and of non-linear responses, are expected to increase rapidly'. See www.worldwatch. org/files/pdf/SOWO9-chap2.pdf

'They say that since the industrial revolution and our discovery that by burning fossil fuels we could create almost limitless energy, global temperatures have increased by 0.8°C.'
James Hansen, 'The Threat to the Planet: How can we avoid dangerous human-made climate change?' (2006). See www. columbia.edy/~jeh1/2006/DukeEdin_ complete_20061121.pdf

'We are already seeing the effects of the 8°C rise:

Glaciers retreating in the Himalayas...
Geology News article, 'Himalayan Glacier Retreat Blamed on Global Warming,' January 16th 2007.

Massive shrinking of the Artic Sea Ice...
According to the Climate Safety Report from the Public Interest and Research Centre in 2008 (see http://climatesafety. org/wp-content/uploads/climatesafety.pdf).

Drought in Australia...
Michael Byrnes 'Scientists see Antarctic Vortex as Drought Maker,' Reuters 23rd September 2003

$150 billion a year of damage from natural catastrophes...
UN Environment Program see www.unep.org

Floods in Bangladesh putting 80% of the country under 2m of water....
James Martin *The Meaning of the 21st Century* (Random House, 2006).

Temperature rises of 3-4°C in Alaska...
See 'What is Happening to the Arctic Climate?' online at www.acia.cicero.uio.no/factsheets/1_arctic_climate_trends.pdf

Sea-level rises of 3.1mm per year since 1993...
Stefan Rahmstorf et al, 'Recent climate observations compared to projections,' Science 316 (5825), May 4th 2007, p.709.

300,000 extra deaths a year from higher temperatures, which cause the spread of disease.'
For more on Kofi Annan's Global Humanitarian Forum 2009 see www.commondreams.org/headline/2009/05/29

'When we go over 1°C (that's a "when" not an "if")...
Or maybe 2°C or more? James Hansen et al 'Target Atmospheric CO2: Where Should Humanity Aim?' (2008) at www.columbia.edu/~jeh1/2008/TargetCO2_20080407.pdf

...there'll be no ice on Mount Kilimanjaro, the ecosystem around the Great Barrier Reef will completely collapse and hundreds of island nations will be uninhabitable.'
Rob Hopkins *The Transition Handbook* (Green Books, 2008).

'If we reach 2°C the WWF thinks the Greenland ice sheet will go into meltdown resulting in a 7m sea level rise, putting most coastal cities under water.'

'Currently, more than 200 million people live in coastal floodplains around the world, with two million square kilometres of land and one trillion dollars worth of assets less than one metre elevation above current sea level. A quarter of Bangladesh's population (thirty-five million people) lives within the coastal floodplain. Many of the world's major cities (twenty-two of the top fifty) are at risk of flooding from coastal surges, including Tokyo, Shanghai, Hong Kong, Mumbai, Kolkata, Karachi, Buenos Aires, St Petersburg, New York, Miami and London. In almost every case, the city relies on costly flood defenses for protection. Even if protected, these cities would lie below sea level with a residual risk of flooding like New Orleans today. The homes of tens of millions more people are likely to be affected by flooding from coastal storm surges with rising sea levels. People in South and East Asia will be most vulnerable, along with those living on the coast of Africa and on small islands.'

Nicholas Stern, *The Economics of Climate Change: The Stern Review* (Cambridge University Press, 2006), p.90.

'3°C will see the Amazon ecosystem collapse, making it the greatest emitter of CO2 in the world, as trees die and forest fires rage through the landscape.'

David Spratt, *'The Big Melt: Lessons from the Arctic Summer of 2007,'* Carbon Equity (2007). See www.carbonequity.info

---

'There's been a lot of confusion about climate change. Some of it has been real scientific debate, a lot of it has been generated by paid-up climate deniers funded by Exxon Mobile, who wanted to rock people's faith in science so that they'd buy more cigarettes.'

George Monbiot, *Heat: How To Stop the Planet Burning* (Penguin Books, 2006).

'CO2 concentrations (in parts per million) for the last 1100 years...'

This graph is from David Mackay *Sustainable Energy: Without Hot Air* (UIT, 2009). See www.withouthotair.com

---

'Sunspots affect the temperature on earth.'

It's actually extra bright spots that cause warming. These go in eleven year cycles, and they don't show a steady upward or downward trend. So the warming of the last forty years must be something else. Claims that they do are refuted here: Eos, Vol.85, No.39, September 28th 2004, 'Pattern of Strange Errors Plagues Solar Activity and Terrestrial Climate Data,' see http://stephenschneider. stanford.edu/Publications/PDF_Papers/ DamonLaut2004.pdf

---

'Sulphur emissions banned twenty years ago are still high in the atmosphere, blocking sunlight and helping cool the earth.'

The atmospheric haze from sulphur emissions banned twenty years ago has been blocking sunlight and helping cool the earth. Nobel Peace Prize winner Professor Paul Crutzen helped ban CFCs but now says that they help with global cooling and we may need to launch sulphur rockets into the troposphere (2007). See http://news.bbc.co.uk/1/hi/ programmes/6369971.stm

---

'The arctic sea ice may be gone in a couple of summers' time.'

Louis Fortier, scientific director of the Canadian research network ArcticNet, believes that the ocean could be ice-free in summertime as soon as 2010. NASA climate scientist Jay Zwally says 2012. See http://climatesafety.org/ wp-content/uploads/climatesafety.pdf

'Why don't we trust climate scientists just because they're only 95% sure climate change is man-made?'

According to the Climate Safety Report 2008 (http://climatesafety.org/wp-content/uploads/climatesafety.pdf) 1990 growth levels were 1.1% a year and last year they grew by 3%.

....

'One last thing: beneath any article on the environment you'll find someone, if not ten people, telling you that climate change is a huge conspiracy.'

For examples of climate deniers see the World Climate Report found online at www.worldclimatereport.com: 'Climate change is a largely overblown issue and that the best expectation is modest change over the next 100 years'.

──────────────

CHAPTER 2

'The stories that my environmentalist friends would tell about rising temperatures, melting ice-caps and ever-decreasing rainforests were probably true, but I hoped that the government would have it all in hand.'

See David Wasdell, Feedback Dynamics and the Acceleration of Climate Change: An Update of the Scientific Analysis (2007) at www.meridian.org.uk/_PDFs/FeedbackDynamics.pdf

....

In the summer of 2007, scientists monitoring the Arctic sea ice shocked the world with the pictures they produced. From one year to the next it had shrunk by 1.5 million square kilometres – that's an area nearly three times the size of France. But in some ways 2008 was even worse.'

These statistics regarding the shrinking of Arctic Ice are from the National Snow and Ice Data Centre. See http://seensidc.org/news/press/20081002_seaice_pressrelease.html which cites the decrease is as follows:
2007 - 4.28 million square kilometers.
2008 - 4.67 million square kilometers

....

'The previous year there were perfect melting conditions – clear skies and high temperatures. 2008 was a lot cooler. The Arctic sea ice recovered a bit, but not much, even though the conditions were ideal for ice to grow...'

Discussing the perfect melting conditions, good ice formation conditions, the NSIDC Research Scientist Julienne Stroeve said: 'I find it incredible that we came so close to beating the 2007 record – without the especially warm and clear conditions we saw last summer. I hate to think what 2008 might have looked like if weather patterns had set up in a more extreme way.' National Snow and Ice Data Centre press release of October 2nd 2008 found at http://nsidc.org/news/press/20081002_seaice_pressrelease.html

....

'...and even though it [the Arctic Ice] covered a larger area, it was thinner and so the total mass was actually the smallest it has ever been.'

In 2008, the NSIDC reported that summer sea ice area recovered by 9% but was still the second lowest recorded. However, based on the latest data about the much greater area of thin first-year ice and losses of multi-year ice, especially that of five years or more, they believe that in volume terms last summer was the lowest since records began in the 1930s – and probably for at least 700 years and possibly up to 8,000 years, said Walt Meier, a research scientist at the Boulder-based centre.

'Our estimate is that it was probably the lowest volume on record,' Meier told *The Guardian* (April 6th 2009) 'Certainly 2007 and 2008 [were] the two lowest [years for] volume and extent.' (See www.guardian.co.uk/environment/2009/apr/06/arctic-sea-ice-warning.

'The Climate Safety Report, published in 2008, now predicts there will be no sea ice by summer 2015, and this might even happen as early as 2011.'
See http://climatesafety.org/wp-content/uploads/climatesafety.pdf

'The Arctic sea ice works like a huge fridge for the whole northern hemisphere and as it grows warmer the whole area will become warmer too.'
The Albedo Effect states that white ice is a reflective surface, see the Climate Safety Report 2008 (as above) p.8.

'The permafrost in the Arctic Circle is frozen ground containing millions of tonnes of greenhouse gases. If it all melts it will triple the carbon dioxide in the atmosphere, massively increasing global warming.'
Permafrost would triple GHGs according to the Climate Safety Report 2008, p.8. Recent research has shown that permafrost contains twice as much carbon as previously thought: in total 1,672 billion tonnes of carbon worldwide, equivalent to more than double the 750 billion tonnes in the atmosphere at the moment (total manmade emissions since 1850 are 340 billion tonnes). We don't know how much of that is methane, twenty-five times more powerful than CO2.

'Although the sea ice won't cause a sea level rise by itself, it could lead to the irreversible decline of the Greenland ice sheet, leading to a 7m rise.'
Some cite the potential sea-level rise as around 4 inches. This is not accurate, as when the sea level rises it displaces as much water as it replaces when it melts: the Greenland ice-sheet allegedly holds 6% of all fresh water on the planet and a 7m sea level rise is cited by the Climate Safety Report 2008, p.10.

'It may be too late to save the Arctic sea ice. We may have no choice but to try huge geo-engineering projects, like spraying sulphur high into the atmosphere to reflect sunlight, in order to make the ice form again.'
For more on Professor Stephen Salter's plans for new sulphur sprays see 'Futurist Fleet of Cloudseers' by Professor John Latham, BBC News, February 2007, online at www.news.bbc.co.uk/2/hi/programmes/6354759.stm

'It's the biggest coal-fired power station in Europe and the site of the first ever Climate Camp.'
See http://news.bbc.co.uk/1/hi/england/north_yorkshire/5300560.stm

---

'In my imaginary paradise, the water that I flush down my toilet would not be a fifth of the water I use each day, but if that means compost toilets I don't want to be the girl in charge of them.'
See http://americancityandcounty.com/mag/government_tapping_water_shortage

---

'The girl mentioned a phone call she'd had from her Mum, worried sick after reading news reports that the camp was full of terrorists.'
See www.telegraph.co.uk/news/worldnews/1560253/Heathrow-climate-protest-grows-by-the-hour.html

---

'I thought about her grandchildren growing up under the flight path, with the deafeningly loud planes passing overhead every ninety seconds.'
See www.cpresurrey.org.uk/xhtml/news/heathrow_jan08.html

'I knew that expanding Heathrow would make it the UK's single biggest emitter of CO2.'
See www.greenpeace.org.uk/files/pdfs/climate/case-against-heathrow-expansion.pdf

---

CHAPTER 3

'I reminded him that a hundred and sixty thousand people were already dying each year from diseases that had spread because of rising temperatures.'

See http://fire.pppl.gov/aaas04_king_final.pdf

'When you think about all the big historic movements, from the Suffragettes, to anti-apartheid, to sexual equality in the 1960s, all the big political movements had popular mobilization. Maybe it's an odd thing for someone in government to say, but I just think there's a real opportunity and a need here.'
Ed Miliband
See www.telegraph.co.uk/news/newstopics/politics/labour/3681149/Ed-Miliband-urges-popular-mobilisation-to-tackle-climate-change.html

---

'Aviation is not the biggest emitter of carbon. In fact, it is responsible for less than 5% of global greenhouse emissions...'
For the 'Aviation and Climate Change' report from the US Government Accountability Office (2009) see www.gao.gov/products/GAO-09-554

'That's much less than livestock (22%)...'
Fertiliser used to produce livestock feed contributes 22% to global gas emissions (see www.brass.cf.ac.uk/uploads/271005_TGpres.pdf).

'And much less than rice cultivation (18%).'
http://www.methanetomarkets.org/events/2009/all/docs/all-27jan09/subcommittee/ag/enteric_rice_26jan.pdf

'It [the aviation industry] is growing really fast and will contribute 15% of greenhouse gases worldwide each year by 2050.'
See the Intergovernmental Panel on Climate Change at www.ipcc.ch

'75% of European flights are leisure trips.'
John Stewart, Chair of Hacan (an anti-aviation NGO).

'Nearly 50% of all flights in Europe are under 500km.'
Havant Friends of the Earth -
see www.havantfoe.org.uk.

'Air travel is nineteen times more polluting that train travel.'
www.energybulletin.net/node/6372

'The top ten most popular destinations from Heathrow include Paris, Amsterdam, Glasgow and Edinburgh.'
See Martin McCauley's article on the top destinations from Heathrow Airport in 2009 at www.ezinearticles.com/ ?Heathrow-Airport-Destinations&id

'If Europe continues on current trends the EU's entire carbon budget will be taken up solely by aviation by 2040.'
See 'Pace Hots up by a World Forever On the Move,' by Anthony Barnett at www. guardian.co.uk22. www.greenpeace.org. uk/tags/stansted?page=1

'The average British person has a carbon footprint of 11 tonnes of CO2 for a whole year.'

See www.independent.co.uk/environment/ climate-change/your-carbon-footprint-revealed-climate-change-report-finds-we-each-produce-11-tons-of-carbon-a-year--and-breaks-down-how-we-do-it-427664.html

'One return flight to Australia produces nearly 7 tonnes.'
www.chroniclelive.co.uk/north-east-news/the-environment/go-green-news/2009/02/03/carbon-emissions-facts-bring-us-down-to-earth-72703-22842479/

'You can change all your light bulbs, unplug all your phone chargers, take all your appliances off standby and recycle religiously and one flight will cancel all those savings out.'
John Stewart, Chair of Hacan (an anti-aviation NGO).

'We're most famous for projects like the book Change the World for a Fiver and the "I'm not a plastic bag" shopping bag.'
Change the World for a Fiver (Short Books, 2008)

CHAPTER 4

In 2006 five times as many American women had breast enlargement operations than in 2005.
Jean Twenge, The Narcissism Epidemic: Living in the Age of Entitlement (Free Press, 2009).

Teenage girls have seen a huge rise in mental health problems.
Oliver James, Britain on the Couch (Arrow, 1998), updated edition forthcoming.

'70% of the world's poor are women.'
P.T. Denton in Rachel Masika, *Gender, Development and Climate Change* (Oxfam Publishing, 2002).

....

'75% of environmental refugees are women.'
M. Monirul Qader Mirza, *'Climate Change and Extreme Weather Events: can developing countries adapt?'* *Climate Policy*, vol 3, Issue 3 (available online at www.sciencedirect.com).

....

85% of the victims of climate-induced disasters are women.'
See *UN Refugees* magazine, vol 1, #126 (2002).

....

'Across the world, where women have been taught to read the birth rate has dropped dramatically. Protecting and empowering women is a central part of the solution to climate change.'
Countries which have a higher proportion of women in government have ratified more environmental treaties (Norgaard and York, 'Gender Equality and State Environmentalism,' Gender & Society, vol 19, #4, 2005). 80% of women are very concerned about climate change according to the Women's Manifesto on Climate Change produced by the Women's Environmental Network and the National Federation of Women's Institutes (15th May 2007).

....

'The world I was brought up in taught me that empowerment meant finding out what I really wanted... But all I was supposed to 'really want'

was an endless catalogue of things: holidays in beautiful places, the perfect pair of shoes, the colour coordinated i-phone.'
In the UK, women spend more time shopping than men (see Office of National Statistics Time Use Survey 2005, www.statistics.gov.uk) and make the majority of purchases that have a direct impact on climate change, including food, clothing and household goods (Office of National Statistics Expenditure and Food Survey 2006, as above). As household managers, they are also key to controlling the 30% of UK carbon emissions that are produced in the home (Energy Saving Trust, 2007).

CHAPTER 5

'Some people use peak oil to mean the moment when half of all the oil in the world has been extracted'
Rob Hopkins, *Transition Handbook* (Green Books, 2008).

'Some say it's when the amount we're using is more than we can get out of the ground.'
The Peak Oil Group or UK Industry Taskforce on Peak Oil and Energy Security includes AWP, FirstGroup, Foster& Partners, Scottish and Southern Energy, Solarcentury, Stagecoach Group, Virgin Group and Yahoo.
See www.peakoiltaskforce.net.

'In 2006 the International Energy Agency said that people talking about Peak Oil were "scare-mongerers".'

In the foreword to the International Energy Agency report in 2005, executive director Claude Mandil, dismissed those who warned of this event as 'doomsayers'. He writes: 'The IEA has long maintained that none of this is a cause for concern,' in 'Resources to Reserves: Oil and Gas Technologies for the Energy Markets of the Future.' IEA report 2005 (see page 3).

'Its 2008 report said that world production of conventional oil would peak or plateau in 2020.'
'Although global oil production in total is not expected to peak before 2030, production of conventional oil…is projected to level off towards the end of the projection period,' according to the IEA report 2008 in *'World Energy Outlook 2008'* (see page 43). In conversation with George Monbiot, Fatih Birol states:

'In terms of non-OPEC [countries outside the big oil producers' cartel], we are expecting that in three, four years' time the production of conventional oil will come to a plateau, and start to decline… In terms of the global picture, assuming that OPEC will invest in a timely manner, global conventional oil can still continue, but we still expect that it will come around 2020 to a plateau as well, which is of course not good news

from a global oil supply point of view.' See www.monbiot.com/archives/2008/12/15/at-last-a-date

'CEOs of BP and Conoco have given the date of the peak between 2010 and 2020.'
www.logicalscience.com/energy/quotes.html

'Dr Colin Campbell, former chief geologist and vice-president of BP, Shell, Fina, Exxon and ChevronTexaco says that the peak of cheap oil happened in 2005, while the peak of harder to extract forms of oil will come in 2011.'
Dr Colin Campbell on peak oil dates see www.oilcrisis.com/de/lecture.html

'The Peak Oil Group, a set of British companies including Virgin, Yahoo and Scottish and Southern Energy, commissioned a report on peak oil. They concluded the peak would arrive in 2013.'
See www.peakoiltaskforce.net

'In Britain most of our farmland is so poor that pretty much nothing grows without the aid of fertilizers made from oil.'
See Rebecca Hoskin's documentary *A Farm for the Future*, BBC2 (2009).

''Actually, the solution to one is the solution to both.'
For more on thinking about peak oil and climate change together, see Bryn Davidson at www.dynamiccities.squarespace.com

'We have to have local communities that can produce lots of their own food and energy, don't rely on long supply chains and are still connected to

other communities but not so dependent on them.'
Rob Hopkins, *Transition Handbook*
(Green Books, 2008).

. . . .

'My housemate is involved in Hackney
Transition Town. She organises seedling swaps
and environmental film screenings...'
See the Transition Town Hackney
website at http://tthackney.org

CHAPTER 6

'Airports up for expansion...'
For more on the planned expansion
for various UK airports see www.
greenpeace.org.uk/files/pdfs/climate/
case-against-heathrow-expansion.pdf

. . . .

'Your local RBS-NatWest 'Since we became
shareholders they have been involved in financing
loans to coal, oil and gas companies worth nearly
£10 billion – over 50% of the amount that the
bank has received from us.'
See www.banktrack.org/download/the_
oil_gas_bank_rbs_the_financing_of_
climate_change/0_1_1_0_0_070312rbs_
oil_gas_bank.pdf

. . . .

'Get in touch with the Robin Hood spirit,
remind yourself of whose money's being used to
fund the fossil fuel industry (70% of it is your
money) and whose future their investments
put at risk.'
See http://business.timesonline.co.uk/
tol/business/industry_sectors/banking_
and_finance/article6051051.ece

. . . .

'In May 1994, after a secret meeting with Shell,
the Nigerian Head of Internal Security called
for 'ruthless military operations'. The result?
Dozens of villages destroyed, thousands of
people made homeless and hundreds massacred.
Shell has even admitted that it supplied guns
for these "security operations".'
See www.ratical.org/corporations/
OgoniFactS.html

. . . .

'Local Government: "What can a council do to
tackle climate change?" Alexis Rowell, Liberal
Democrat councillor for Camden'
For more on Alexis Rowell's proposals
for local councils tackling climate change
see www.carbonchallenge.typepad.com

CHAPTER 7

'Some people, like Danish academic and
environmental writer Bjorn Lomborg, think that
getting the third world out of poverty should be
our number one priority.'
Bjorn Lomborg, *Cool It: The Skeptical
Environmentalist's Guide to Global Warming*
(Knopf, 2007).

. . . .

'Rice crops decline 10% for every 1°C
temperature rise. For half the world it makes up
80% of their food.'
See 'Rice Yields Decline with Higher
Night Temperature from Global
Warming,' by Shaobing Peng et al,
contributed by Gurdev S. Khush to the
Proceedings of the National Academy of
Sciences, May 27th 2004, at www.pnas.
org/content/101/27/9971.full

'Nicholas Stern, economist and academic, says we have three problems on our hands: poverty, climate change and the economic crisis. They are linked and cannot be thought about or tackled separately.'
Nicholas Stern, *A Blueprint for a Safer Planet* (The Bodley Head, 2009).

'Oliver Tickell...has the idea that carbon trading can work, if we charge people at the source (so at the coal mine or the oil rig), have lots of improved legislation to close up loopholes and keep a really clear idea of what the money raised is going to be used for.'
See Oliver Tickell, *Kyoto 2* (Zed Books, 2008).

'...it would be a lot better than the current levels of poverty experienced by the third of people in the world currently living on $2 a day.'
Two billion people in the world currently live on $2 a day, according to World Development Indicators, Washington: World Bank (2005), see http://devdata.worldbank.org/wdi2005/cover.htm

RESOURCES

If you want to find out more...

READ ~ Top 3 books for learning about climate change

Mark Lynas, *Six Degrees: Our Future on a Hotter Planet* (Fourth Estate, 2007), provides a very graphic description of what the world will look like the temperature rises.

David Mackay, *Sustainable Energy: Without Hot Air* (UIT, 2009). The most up-to-date and trustworthy source of information on how to get the country weaned off fossil fuels. It's free and constantly updated online at www.withouthotair.com

George Marshall, *Carbon Detox: Your Step-by-step Guide to Getting Real About Climate Change* (Gaia Books, 2007), includes practical and entertaining advice on how to overcome climate denial and 'drop a tonne' off your carbon footprint.

READ ~ Top 3 books about activism

Trenna Cormack, *Be The Change: Action and Reflection from People Transforming Our World* (Love Books Ltd, 2007). A series of interviews with ordinary people who have decided to change the world.

Ann Charters, *The Portable Sixties Reader* (Penguin Classics, 2002). Inspirational stories, articles and essays from the revolutionary movements of the 1960s – civil rights, women's rights, the sexual revolution, environmentalists, anti-war protestors...

Liz McQuiston, *Suffragettes to She-devils* (Phaidon Press, 1997). A compilation of beautiful, rare and hard-hitting images charting the last hundred years of the women's movement all over the world.

READ ~ Top 3 books about feminism

Naomi Klein, *No Logo* (Flamingo, 2001). Still super-relevant now, nearly ten years after it was first published, the book has some enlightening things to say about why feminism seems to have disappeared (especially Chapter 5, *'The Patriarchy Gets Funky'*). The basic premise is that branding is a new form of advertising that has commodified everything – including the identities that spent the 70s and 80s subversively challenging consumerism.

Ariel Levy, *Female Chauvanist Pigs* (Free Press, 2005). Looks at the rise of raunch culture in the USA and assesses whether a whole generation of women modelling themselves on porn stars really does constitute a new form of feminism. (At the risk of spoiling it for you, she thinks it doesn't.)

Susie Orbach, *Bodies* (Profile Books, 2009). Most people in the West no longer have any direct relationship with their food, their clothes or the tools and technologies they use every day. Instead, we – both men and women, but women especially – seem to have turned on our bodies as things to be 'worked on' and 'made'. Susie draws on her experience as a psychoanalyst to put contemporary women's body issues in the wider context of western discomfort with bodies and their limitations.

WATCH ~ Top 3 films about climate change

Home (2009) directed by Yann Arthus Betrand and produced by Luc Besson. A beautiful and frightening film about our relationship with the planet using aerial footage from all around the world.

The Age of Stupid (2009) directed by Franny Armstrong. It's 2055 and Pete Postlethwaite is the last man on earth, looking back at 2007 and trying to work out why we didn't stop climate change when we knew it was coming.

The Plan (2009). Swedish documentary-makers have travelled the world seeking the people with the ideas that could change the world and save society. Released December 2009 this film will be screened at Copenhagen. Let's hope the international community learns something.

WATCH ~ Top 3 films about activism

Milk (2008) directed by Gus Van Sant and starring Sean Penn. A biopic about the life and assassination of gay rights activist Harvey Milk.

Taking Liberties (2007) by Chris Atkins is a hilarious and shocking documentary about how far our civil liberties have been curtailed under New Labour.

The Power of Community: How Cuba Survived Peak Oil (2006) by Faith Morgan is a documentary about Cuba's amazing adaptation to life without oil in the 1990s.

VIRAL ~ not got time for a whole film?

5 minutes: *DeSmog TV* at www.desmogblogblog.com follow the fight against climate science myths

10 minutes: www.wakeupfreakout.org animation on tipping points, feedback mechanisms, and why the time to act is now.

20 minutes: *A Time Comes: The Story of the Kingsnorth Six* (2009) by Nick Broomfield

In 2007 six Greenpeace activists climbed up the stacks at Kingsnorth power station, abseiled down the side and started graffiti-ing 'Gordon Bin It'. When it came to court they were acquitted because of the harm climate change does to the planet…a really inspiring story of a landmark case. For a free copy of the dvd to host your own screening and share the film with your friends/family/community see www.greenpeace.org.uk/ atimecomes/host-your-own-screening-order

GET ACTIVE ~ The Climate Rush isn't the only activist group you can get involved with, here's 5 more:

Climate Camp www.climatecamp.org.uk
An annual camp taking sustainable living to the doorstep of the big carbon polluters. This year sees the first Climate Camps in Scotland and Wales, and a Bristol co-mutiny.

Plane Stupid www.planestupid.com
A single issue campaign group taking direction action against aviation expansion and short haul flights. There are groups in London, Glasgow, Brighton, Manchester, Southhampton, Leeds, Edinburgh and Cambridge.

Rising Tide www.risingtide.org.uk
A network of environmental activist groups with bases in Bristol, Cleveland & Whitby, Cornwall, Hastings, Leamington Spa, London, Mid-Walles, Norwich, Plymouth, Reading Scotland, Sheffield and Worthing.

Coal Action Network www.leaveitintheground.org.uk
A network of groups campaigning against coal – the dirtiest fuel and the biggest historical cause of climate change.

Biofuelwatch www.biofuelwatch.org.uk
This organisation campaigns against biofuels, which can be several hundred times worse than oil.

SURF ~ 3 fun sites for the future

www.ecomotion.org.uk: A networking site for individuals and organisations.

www.envirowiki.info: A '*wikipedia*' for the environmental movement.

www.indiaclimatesolutions.com: All over India people are coming up with amazing grass-roots solutions to climate change and environmental problems.

ACTION ~ Top 3 things to do if you want to do a bit:

- Go veggie for the day; as suggested by Paul McCartney's campaign for 'Veggie Mondays'.
- Cut down on buying stuff – organise swap shops etc. instead
- Avoid flying, especially domestically

Top 3 things to do if you want to do some more:

- Cut out meat and cut down on animal products
- Make sure your workplace is as environmentally-friendly as possible
- Get your bike out

Top 3 things to do if you want to do loads:

- Go vegan (I haven't managed this yet...but I'll get there one day!)
- Join the Climate Rush
- Stop flying